People of God,
Peoples of
God

Edited by **Hans Ucko**

People of God,
Peoples of
God

A Jewish-Christian
Conversation in Asia

WCC Publications, Geneva

Cover design: Rob Lucas

ISBN 2-8254-1172-8

© 1996 WCC Publications, World Council of Churches,
150 route de Ferney, 1211 Geneva 2, Switzerland

Printed in Switzerland

Contents

Introduction: Jews and Asian Christians — Reasons for Encounter

HANS UCKO

"Banana" and "coconut" are names Asian and African Christians sometimes use ironically to describe their own predicament. From the outside one may look like any other ordinary Chinese, Indian or African man or woman, but inside, under the yellow peeling or brown shell, the difference appears: the fruit is as white as the skin of a Western Christian. Asian or African Christians may look Asian or African, but their faith, that which constitutes them, is seen as something coming from outside, from their white and Western former masters and colonizers. Christianity is regarded as a Western religion, brought to Asia to conquer the religions of Asia. Little does it help to point out that Christianity, with its roots in Judaism, was actually born in Asia, for the Christianity which became known in Asia was manifestly a white, Western religion that had little to do with its Asian origins.

Alienation and identity

There is pain in being looked upon as a stranger in one's own context, in being, like the banana or the coconut, different on the inside from the outside. Or as a Chinese Christian once put it, "The whites are ghosts, we Chinese Christians are the yellow ghosts." The images vary, but the message is the same. Before the coming of the missionaries, before they became Christians, they were part and parcel of their community and people. Becoming Christian meant changing — the church called it becoming a new person — which is quite possible. But it also meant — which no one said — that one was taken out of one's own culture. One experienced a twofold conversion: first a conversion to Christianity, then the conversion to Western culture. Suddenly one's Chinese or Indian culture became a problem.

There was alienation. Chinese Christians began to look upon themselves as having two identities in one person, on the one hand struggling to retain their identity as Chinese and on the other hand being Christian. Having two identities can create a problem, particularly if they are in conflict with each other.

There are stories of Chinese families newly converted to Christianity burning the image of the dragon in the courtyard as a victory for the church, yet what they were burning was really not the Christian symbol of Satan or the devil, but the ancient Chinese symbol of fertility, goodness and prosperity, the life-force itself. Indian Christians tell similar stories. They were and sometimes still are looked upon as aliens. They may be Indians in blood and colour, but they are considered white in their thinking and are thus strangers, foreigners, who do not belong.

Jewish history is replete with experiences of not belonging. The reasons may not be the same. Asian Christians became in some important ways estranged from their own people in accepting a Christianity that was not separated from Western civilization and culture. The early mission enterprise placed an equal-sign between Christianity and Western civilization. Asian Christians may have wondered why faith in Christ required them to become what they were not and never could be — Western Christians.

The Jewish community was called by the covenant in the desert to live a Jewish life in all its various facets, and the world around them could not stand it. As Lewis John Eron writes, "The Jews can only be understood as the eternal *doppelgänger* to the predominant Christian culture of the West. Jewish culture is the threatening yet unseen ghost whose very presence challenges the assumption that Jesus of Nazareth is necessarily the central figure of Western culture."[1] Jews have experienced being strangers and felt the burden of not belonging in Christian Europe.

Over the centuries, the two faith traditions, Jewish and Christian, have had to live near one another in Europe. It was not easy living together, particularly after the Christian church acquired power from its alliance with the worldly powers in the form of the Roman empire. For the Jewish community European history cannot be dissociated from the experience of segregation, exclusion, ghetto and discrimination, coming to its peak in this century during the Nazi era in central

Europe. The Shoah (Holocaust) was the absolutization of the exclusion of the Jewish people. The deep tragedy from the Christian point of view is that the Nazi attempt at a "final solution" did not come as a bolt from the blue, but out of a long period of deliberate efforts by Christians to prove their sole right to the heritage of the covenant between God and Abraham, an attempt that goes by the name "replacement theology", according to which the church has replaced Israel as the new people of God, the new Israel, the true Israel.

Since the Enlightenment Europe has been asking the same question, "Are Jews part of the nation or not? Can they be? Where is their allegiance? Are they more German, French, British than they are Jewish?" And Jews in turn will ask, "Can Jews in France today be assured that they are considered to be as French as anyone else? Am I a French national who happens to be a Jew, or am I a Jew who lives in a certain part of Europe?" The answer is interrelated with one's understanding of Jewish identity.

So although they are very different from each other, the Jewish community in Europe and the Christian community in Asia have had to reflect in a similar way on the significance of their particular identity. For Asian Christians could just as well ask themselves whether they are Asians with a Christian identity or Christians who happen to live in Asia.

Jews have been anxious not to lose their identity as a distinct community. Their religious tradition, culture and social network have provided guidance and inspiration, safety and security; and they have seen it as worthwhile to hold on to that. They have not considered society at large as something worthy of being assimilated to. Only in the 20th century has it become for some increasingly attractive to assimilate and let go of the distinctiveness of the Jewish community.

Living with Western Christendom

Through the missionary enterprise Asian Christians have inherited a faith that has upheld them, given guidance and inspiration, provided safety and security. And yet they have not found a satisfactory way of being as Christians fully part of their own culture and tradition. How can they as Christians in Asia come home to Asian cultures and traditions?

The struggles towards emancipation from the colonial yoke in many countries in Asia were accompanied by attempts on the part of Asian theologians to liberate Christian faith from the missionary yoke and move towards a reconciliation between Asian cultural traditions and Christian identity. Some way or other Asian Christians needed to look for a Christianity that could stand on its own feet and build its own foundation in Asia.

Asian Christians share with other Christians a context that has been anxious to preserve a distinct tradition, in which the stories of Abraham, Isaac and Jacob, the Exodus event, the Israelite kingdoms, the prophets, the Wisdom literature, the Psalms, the books of Ruth and Job have been formative factors. Hebron, Jerusalem, Nazareth, Mount Zion, the Sea of Galilee, the River Jordan — all are well-known places in this faith perspective. This is the heritage. To the River Ganges one brings along, as it were, a piece of geography from another part of the world and calls it "Holy Land geography". To the world of Confucius and Lao-tse one brings along a part of history from another people and calls it salvation history. Christian mission brought Jesus Christ — someone from the "Holy Land" and from "salvation history" — and people in India and China took to him and began calling themselves Christians. But there was not much space left over for the Ganges or Lao-tse.

A Jewish sage once said bitterly, "The greatest tragedy that ever came upon the Jewish people was not the exile in Babylon or the destruction of the temple. It was the day when seventy old men locked themselves up in Alexandria and translated our holy scriptures into Greek." True, the world came to know the Jewish people and its history through the Septuagint, the Greek translation of the Hebrew Scriptures (Old Testament). At the same time, however, the history of the Jewish people became the property of everyone and thus open to any interpretation. And the Christian reading of the Old Testament would eventually interpret it as speaking against its own people, the Jews.

At first glance, Christians in the South and Jews in the North have very different experiences. Jews have lived and in a way shared a culture with Western Christians which has nevertheless left them bitter memories of ghetto, burning of the Talmud and forced baptism. Even if things look different today — the Inquisition is long gone and freedom of religion is guaranteed — Western society, despite increasing secularization, remains deeply rooted in a Christian culture. In the Jewish mind, Christians are still identified with power, influence and majority.

Except in the Philippines, Asian Christians are minorities in their respective countries. They live as Christians in the midst of very strong cultures, which have given birth to the Hindu, Buddhist, Confucian and Taoist traditions and religions. With some exceptions, they received the Christian faith from the West. Parallel with the liberation from the colonizing powers in this century there has been a movement to make Christianity in Asia truly Asian and not only a European implant in the vibrant religious garden of Asia.

What Jews and Asian Christians share is the heritage of living at the mercy of powerful Western Christendom. This suggests therefore the possibility of comparing notes and exchanging experiences. Yet not until recently has the door been open to such common explorations. With few exceptions, the Christian understanding of Judaism has been the same, whether one was a Christian from Rome, Wittenberg or Geneva or from Madras, Guangzhou or Rangoon. Knowledge in Asia about the Jewish people and Judaism is probably more hearsay than first-hand experience and most likely based on what Western missionaries once said. There were few occasions to meet, see and experience living Judaism in Asia.

Since the churches of the South received their formative theological patterns from the churches of the North, they largely took over the replacement theme which had developed strongly in the churches of the North. This created a certain bewilderment in many churches in the South. In many ways mission was an enterprise that emphasized the Bible, which meant a strong attachment to the biblical stories of the Jewish people. On the other hand there was the theological concept that the old covenant between God and Israel had all come to an end with the advent of the church and its proclamation of the gospel of Jesus of Nazareth and the coming of the kingdom of God.

Asian Christians and the Hebrew scriptures

Asian reflections on the identity of Christians took several different directions, from one in which social commitment predominated, to an orientation in which Asia, as the cradle of world religions, became the cornerstone of theological discourse. In India, the Rethinking Group, so called from a book published in Madras in 1938, *Rethinking Christianity in India*, dominated the theological discussion. An outstanding member of this group was judge P. Chenchiah (1886-1959).

Chenchiah was a theologian who wrestled with the geographical and historical biblical heritage of Christianity. Although his theological reflections are truly original, some of his ideas are shared by many Asian Christians. The Old Testament is not a priori a concern for an Asian Christian like Chenchiah: "[it is] not necessary to hold that Old Testament is an integral part of the Christian message."[2] It is not unusual to encounter Asian Christians today who, inspired perhaps by Chenchiah, would prefer the Bhagavadgita or Dhammapada to the Old Testament as their *praeparatio evangelica*. But while one may be anxious as an Asian Christian to be truly part of Hindu or Buddhist culture, it should not be forgotten that no one, Jew, Hindu or Buddhist, will ever appreciate the reduction of their holy scriptures to little more than an entry-way to Christianity.

Chenchiah realized that as long as the emphasis was on the geography and history of Israel, Christianity would remain a stranger in India. In order to make the Christian message truly universal, it was necessary to release Christianity from what he perceived were only historical bonds, to move from fact to spirit. Chenchiah was convinced that the Hindu would rather be in touch with the Logos than with Jesus of Nazareth: "the Hindu is always looking behind Jesus for the idea of which he is the embodiment."[3] He saw a "deep diversity between the Jesus we proclaim and the Christ India needs. We preach Jesus of Nazareth, born thousands of years ago; India needs the living and present Lord. We offered India the Jesus of history; India wants the universal spirit."[4] But he was not unaware of the consequences of his own reflections: if one was "to preach the gospel of the Holy Spirit, what [would] happen to the gospel of Jesus?"[5]

Chenchiah sought a Christianity that could be set free from its captivity in history and geography and thus be readily available for the Indian soul. A wedge had to be driven between the Old Testament and the New Testament. The Old Testament seemed in the church's theological tradition to sanction a narrow salvation history which ruled out the freedom of the Spirit. Citing Marcion, Chenchiah confessed, "As for Jehovah and the Father of Jesus, it requires some audacity not to agree... that they have not even the remotest resemblance with each other."[6]

The Old Testament could not be a tool for building a truly Indian church. The Old Testament belonged to the Jews and should remain so. The Christian West had manifested all too often

> the pontifical way in which Christians have dealt with Old Testament [and how this] may reasonably draw pointed and angry protests from the Jew. [Jews] may be credited to know the genius of their own faith, the meaning of their own prophecies, the face of their own Messiah. It does sound presumptuous for a Christian to teach the Jew what his own religion means.[7]

Obviously there is not much room for any interaction between Jews and Christians if the Old Testament is simply the background for the New Testament, but apart from that only old and void. However, thanks to the Christian-Jewish dialogue there is a growing realization that a Jewish understanding of the Old Testament may have something to offer Christian theological reflection.

The first church was a church of Jews and Gentiles, united in one faith but diverse in its practices. Gentile Christians were not supposed to live by the law of Moses, Jewish Christians were. Suffice it here to recall how anxious Paul was to make it clear to the elders in Jerusalem that he did not, contrary to rumour, "teach all the Jews living among the Gentiles to forsake Moses, [or] not to circumcise their children or observe the customs". He even took a vow so that everyone would "know that there is nothing in what they have been told about you, but that you yourself observe and guard the law" (Acts 21:17-26).

But the church did not remain a church of Jews and Gentiles. It became a Gentile church, and biblical history became a Christian interpretation called salvation history. The Old Testament was indispensable to understanding that Christ is in the line of creation, fall, original sin, the election of a chosen people, its disobedience, its refusal to listen to the prophets of God. This salvation history has no place for the Old Testament in its own right. It serves as an introduction to what is to come. It is old and in itself clearly of lesser value. Nor is there any place for people of other faiths, unless they acquiesce in seeing themselves as sinners in need of redemption and enter salvation history naked, bereft of their religious traditions. There is no room for their stories, their spiritual experience, their knowledge of the divine presence.

In fact, Chenchiah's protest against the privilege of the Old Testament seems directed less against the Old Testament than against the church's use of it as the only entrance ticket to the Christ-story, thus declaring void any other religious experience. He might have been surprised to learn that the people of the Old Testament are probably even more resentful than he of the way their holy scripture has been used as the vehicle for a Christian salvation story.

Christians have in recent dialogue with Jews sought to understand the Old Testament in its historical setting. Greater hermeneutical sophistication has enabled Christians to hear the Old Testament on its own terms and not in stereotypes:

> Christians in the West "co-opted" the Hebrew scriptures, and over the years have interpreted it in their own way as the "old testament", almost wholly ignoring or rejecting the Jewish interpretations of their own scriptures. But the Jews surely have not surrendered their scriptures to the Christians. The Torah is very much alive, sustaining the life of a persecuted people. Only during recent years has the Jewish interpretation of their own scriptures slowly come to be recognized, at least by some Christian scholars. Admittedly, the relationship between the Hebrew scriptures and the Christian faith is far more intimate and theologically significant than that between the Christian faith and the scriptures of other faiths in Asia. No serious Asian scholar has denied this fact. But few Asian scholars have asked the question, In what ways might the hermeneutical tools of our neighbours be of help in interpreting the Bible to our people in our own cultural context...?[8]

Although some Old Testament concepts play a significant role in various Asian contextual theologies today, it is clear that the absence from the Asian context of a Jewish community, and consequently of the experience of a living Jewish-Christian dialogue, limits direct interaction with a Jewish understanding of the Old Testament. Israel Selvanayagam has noted that the "fascinating attempts at a reconstruction of Christology and a new approach to the Old Testament in the third world coincide with a new approach to the Jewish people and their tradition".[9] So far, however, these concerns have only coincided, not yet intersected. This book seeks to provide space for such an encounter.

The need for encounter

Jews and Asian Christians may need to discover how much different the other is from what one imagined at the outset. Most Asian Christians will no doubt suppose that Jewish-Christian dialogue has little if anything to do with Asia, but is rather a concern for Europe and North America, where there have been and still are Jewish communities. On this view Jewish-Christian dialogue is understood as a commitment to mending the ills of European history, to struggling against antisemitism, to building together a new society while remembering that only yesterday Jews were killed by a Western society founded on Christian values. Understandably, as an ecumenical document says,

> Christians in parts of the world with a history of little or no persecution of Jews do not wish to be conditioned by the specific experiences of justified guilt among other Christians. Rather, they explore in their own ways the significance of Jewish-Christian relations, from the earliest times to the present, for their life and witness. [10]

Asian Christians have no story of a significant Jewish presence in their midst, and antisemitism has hardly been an issue in Asia. Some late 19th-century contacts between East and West may have induced a few Westernized Asians to think in these categories; and King Rama of Thailand brought back from a visit to England a copy of Shakespeare's "The Merchant of Venice" for translation and propagation, though the most that one can probably say about that project is that it was eccentric.

But Jews are by no means strangers to Asia. Both China and India have a long history of Jewish presence. Jews made their home on the southwest coast of India as early as the first century CE, if not before. Many records throughout the centuries attest to the tolerance enjoyed by the Jews of Cochin in south India under Hindu rulers. It was religious sentiment more than anything else that accounted for the first wave of emigration from Cochin to the newly proclaimed state of Israel in 1948; and Indians to this day do not understand why the Indian Jews left for Israel.

Lacking the impetus of living Jewish communities, ordinary Christians in Asia see Judaism as something having more to do with the Bible, something one can find in the Old and New Testaments. Judaism is about the patriarchs and the Promised Land, the kings of Israel and the prophets, the people around Jesus, friends and enemies and Pharisees. More an historical and theological entity than a living faith, Judaism seems to have ended with the destruction of the temple in Jerusalem.

One might also argue that Asian Christians have much more reason to engage in dialogue with Muslims, Hindus and Buddhists than with Jews. They are the real neighbours, with whom there is often too little dialogue and too much communal conflict fuelled by religion. In the light of religious plurality and given the size of the Christian church in Asia, there is real justification for greater interaction on the part of more Christians with their neighbours of other faiths. In a context of communal conflicts Jewish-Christian dialogue seems like a luxury, something only the West can afford.

From the point of view of interfaith relations, churches in the West should reflect on how Jewish-Christian dialogue is perceived in Asia or Africa. Such is the impact and dominance of this dialogue in the interfaith relations of Europe and North America that it almost seems to be a kind of exclusive club where Jews and Christians are together and people of the other faiths are grouped without any particular distinction.

Christians in Asia may also suspect the Jewish-Christian dialogue of being a cover-up which keeps the Israeli-Palestinian issue off the agenda. On this view, Jewish-Christian dialogue becomes a vehicle for promoting Israeli politics. And Christians in Asia, as a minority, have not forgotten the Palestinian Christians. The solidarity that many nations of the South feel with the Palestinians in their conflict with the modern state of Israel may sometimes account for a certain diffidence at the mere mention of Jewish-Christian dialogue.

Jews may need to rethink some of their views of Christians in order to be better equipped for an encounter with Asian Christians. They may need to ask themselves what conditions are required for dialogue with Christians. Can there be a dialogue only when there is common ground? In the West there is certainly ample common ground in the historical experiences of Jews and Christians, which then interact with the more spiritual phenomena to form a solid basis for the dialogue: the biblical ties between Jews and Christians, the Old and the New Testaments. But can there also be a dialogue when there is no common ground? If there is no history of inquisition or antisemitic pogroms, no memories of marginalization in society, is there still reason for encountering the other?

The "Christian world" as most Jews know it is a world where Jews have always been a minority. Despite the vast changes which have made contemporary Europe a pluralistic, secularized, agnostic, materialistic and heterogeneous continent, where church leaders in Europe today call for a Christian home "from the Atlantic to the Urals", Jews remember days when such statements made Jewish communities tremble. Christendom was an all-powerful reality. When church leaders today casually speak of Europe as a Christian continent, it reinforces the conviction that Christianity still equals power — to the detriment of Jewish-Christian dialogue. Can Asian Christians contribute to a changed image of Christianity in the eyes of Jews and people of other faiths? The world of Asian Christians is different. In Asia Christians are a minority. This reality has not so far been part of any Jewish view of Christianity nor of a Jewish-Christian dialogue.

Asian Christians are nourished by the Old Testament and build theologies using motifs from the Old Testament. Conceived in the midst of the reality of the people of Asia, these theologies are usually far away from the findings of Jewish-Christian dialogue. So there may be discoveries to make through an encounter of Jews and Asian Christians. The Taiwanese theologian C.S. Song talks about an "Asian leap", in which the gospel goes straight from Jerusalem to cities and villages in Asia without any detours to the West. He may not have in mind an encounter with the people of the Old Testament, but it is possible that a Jewish reading of the Scriptures could afford a different perspective from the interpretation which had to pass through Athens and Rome on its way to Taipei.

North Atlantic churches dominated the World Council of Churches at the outset. Only from the 1960s onwards did the so-called third world make an impact on ecumenical work. New theological thought-patterns and new modes of spirituality emerged from the other continents and regions — Asia, Latin America and Africa — as a result of the encounter between Christians and people of other faiths.

Deepening intrafaith relations and nurturing interfaith coalitions have produced a new ecumenism. New alignments are possible today, ones which cut through denominations and revolve around the axis of fundamentalist versus progressive. Often disagreements are no longer between faiths or denominations but between those who affirm plurality as a good thing and those who seem to see it as a danger and a threat. For example, Jews and Asian Christians might come to share a similar commitment to religious freedom, given their own experiences in both the past and the present. Such a convergence could open up new horizons, and many living streams of insight could be brought into both intra-Christian conversations and Christian-Jewish dialogue.

Deepening the exchange

This book spans several areas in which Asian Christians and Jews could meet and share experiences. Some of the essays that follow were part of an Asian Christian-Jewish conference held in Cochin in November 1993. In a certain way, the areas covered at the conference and in these articles by Asian Christian and Jewish theologians and scholars belong together. Beyond their specific focus, they all signal a need to continue and deepen the exchange.

Jews and Asian Christians share, as has been said earlier, the experience of being minorities. Jews have lived and continue to live as minorities in Christian- or Muslim-dominated countries. Only since 1948, with the birth of Israel, have Jews experienced being a majority in any country. Christians are a small minority in every Asian country except the Philippines, with its Roman Catholic majority, and South Korea, where Christians may make up as much as one-fourth of the population.

What does it mean to be a minority? If we use a definition from the United Nations, a minority is "a group numerically inferior to the rest of a population of a state, in a non-dominant position, whose members — being nationals of the state — possess ethnic, religious or linguistic characteristics differing from those of the rest of the population and show, if only implicitly, a sense of solidarity, directed towards preserving their culture, traditions, religion or language".[11]

Being a minority is always *in relation*. To use the well-known terminology of Martin Buber, there can be an "I" only if there is a relation to a "Thou". Only in relation to someone else can the "I" very clearly be an "I" and the "Thou" very clearly a "Thou". Does being a minority then depend on the quality of the relation between minority and majority? The constitution of the United States provides a neutral ground for all its citizens irrespective of religious affiliation. The separation between state and church promotes a religious freedom, in which every minority has the freedom of self-expression. While this would seem to be in the interest of the Jewish minority community in the United States, it has also accelerated assimilation and thus been interpreted by some as a threat to the identity of the Jewish community. Does it then follow that a tolerable level of tension between minority and majority, rather than neutrality, is a better climate for the well-being of a minority as a minority? When unconstrained and open relations with the majority are generally possible, how is one to deal with the consequences of declining numbers, inter-marriage and the blurring of boundaries?

Being a minority is not a static phenomenon. A majority may at a certain time or from a certain perspective be considered a minority: for example, Jews are the majority in Israel, but are a minority in the Middle East. Christians are a minority in India, but belong through the Christian fellowship to a world religion which is a majority religion. This is not without consequences. A minority is usually understood as being at the mercy of the majority, powerless in relation to the powerful. But things are not always that simple. The fact that Asian Christians are de facto a minority does not exclude that in some countries they have considerable influence and even control over the majority, being better educated, possessing economic power through the many institutions the colonial powers left in their hands. Provided the means exist, any minority may in a given situation choose — or even feel destined or compelled — to move towards dominance.

Jews and Asian Christians are minorities with a particular claim: they understand themselves to be a people of God. The paradigm of the idea of the people of God, drawn from God's relationship with the people Israel, was also formative for early Christian understanding. As the Christian community grew, its understanding of this original interpretative context was both obscured and informed by other paradigms.

The idea "people of God" can be expressed in different terms and expressions depending on historical and geographical circumstances. One can confess it as the people of God's choice, chosen not for

XX   PEOPLE OF GOD, PEOPLES OF GOD

privilege but obligation, for responsibility to and service of the other. God chose Israel to enter into a particular covenantal relationship, setting the people free in order that they might serve God "as a kingdom of priests and a holy nation". The people of God can be understood as the people of God's calling, the *ekklesia* or the church. In and through Christ, God makes available a new relationship, which draws all races and peoples into covenant with God. Again, especially in contemporary Christian terminology, "people of God" has been understood as the people for whom God is concerned, particularly the poor and the oppressed.

The term "people of God" is communicated best through the language of confession, praise and doxology, to be used primarily in liturgical and devotional contexts, and in offering God's comfort to the community. Such language is not the language of definition but the language of the heart, that is, the language of appellation rather than designation. History records how the proclamation of "people of God" more than once became an instrument of triumphalism indicating nothing but denigration and contempt of the other. It is therefore imperative that the term not be absolutized; it is inherently provisional. The people of God are not an end in themselves (Exodus 19:5; Deuteronomy 7:7). They play a specific role in God's design until the creation itself is set free from its bondage (Romans 8:19-21) and God is all in all (1 Corinthians 15:28).

The Jewish writer Leon Klenicki, reflecting on the significance today of the people of God, says:

> The popular term for the Jews is "The Chosen People". I would prefer to think of us as *a* chosen people... I believe that all people who live a religious life, who have chosen God, are in turn God's people. If we can accept one another's religious vocations we will abolish much of the source of the evil that has infected the world. Will we not then be helping to make the promised kingdom of God a reality? Perhaps it is for this task, the kingdom, that we have *all* been chosen. [12]

At the same time, Asian, African and Latin American theologians are criticizing traditional theology for being too individualistic and unconscious of or indifferent to the peoples and their role in advancing the reign of God. Korean theologian Kim Yong-Bock talks about "the people as subjects of history". It seems as if many of our religious affirmations and declarations need rethinking and reformulation. The affirmations of our religious traditions were conceived in a very different society or situation which is no more. Rather than reflecting on the significance of the otherness of the other, our religious traditions define the other as alien, different, pagan, not belonging, an object over against ourselves as subject. Today we are challenged to rethink in the light of religious plurality the significance of being *a* or *the* people or peoples of God. For what purpose is the concept of the people of God needed? What about other peoples of God? What about the poor and the oppressed as people of God, or those in other cultural and religious traditions who look upon themselves as children of the land, people of God, the *bhummiputras*?

Jewish and Asian Christian reflections emphasize the significance of the people in different yet similar ways. In the Jewish tradition the people shoulder the yoke of salvation at the foot of the mountain, committing themselves to live as a people of God. Salvation is already here; it is not only exodus but it is also becoming a people with a mission in the world. In India a people's theology called Dalit (broken, downtrodden) theology focuses on the injustices that Dalits (the outcastes) suffer. Dalit theology seeks to reinterpret God's liberating presence in a society that denies them their humanity. Ultimately, our questions of liberation from oppressive structures lead us back to the decisive question of who we are in the eyes of God. "We question what we are in the light of an intuitive expectation or a vision of what man ought to be... Something is meant by human being which involves more than just being... We know so little about the humanity of man. We know what he makes, but we do not know what he is." [13]

Jews and Christians derive their anthropology from a shared vision of humankind as the image of God. What does it mean to be created in the image of God? Are there differences between a Christian and a Jewish view? The Jewish tradition is said to be more optimistic as to the potentiality of humankind, while Western Christian theology is said to give more significance to the story of Cain and Abel, the fratricide at the dawn of the human history, as an antidote to any facile discourse on human potentiality.

What additional perspectives might be added to this discussion by Asian Christians drawing on facets and features of the different Asian cultural and religious traditions? As has been said, Asian Christians are increasingly insisting on a recognition of these many and varied traditions. Comparing notes with the Jewish tradition, they would bring out several ideas in seeking the meaning of being the image of God. The Jewish tradition is adamant in refusing to ascribe any holiness to nature and natural objects. God alone is holy, and the God of the Bible is beyond, not within nature. "In the beginning, God created heaven and earth." This would therefore also affect the relationship between the human being and the rest of creation, as the Jewish author Harold Kushner writes: "A Jewish ecology is not based on the assumption that we are no different from other living creatures. It begins with the opposite idea: We have a special responsibility, precisely because we are different."[14] But Taoist, Hindu and Buddhist traditions would paint another image of our interdependent relationship to the environment and finally to Godself. There are ultimately no distinct demarcation lines between the divine and the human, as the following story about the spiritual quest of the "doll of salt" tells us:

> A doll of salt, after a long pilgrimage on dry land, came to the sea and discovered something she had never seen and could not possibly understand. She stood on the firm ground, a solid little doll of salt, and saw there was another ground that was mobile, insecure, noisy, strange and unknown. She asked the sea, "But what are you?", and it said, "I am the sea." And the doll said, "What is the sea?", to which the answer was, "It is me." Then the doll said, "I cannot understand, but I want to; how can I?" The sea answered, "Touch me." So the doll shyly put forward a foot and touched the water and she got a strange impression that it was something that began to be knowable. She withdrew her leg, looked and saw that her toes had gone, and she was afraid and said, "Oh, but where is my toe, what have you done to me?" And the sea said, "You have given something in order to understand." Gradually the water took away small bits of the doll's salt and the doll went farther and farther into the sea and at every moment she had a sense of understanding more and more, and yet of not being able to say what the sea was. As she went deeper, she melted more and more, repeating: "But what is the sea?" At last a wave dissolved the rest of her, and the doll said: "It is I!" She had discovered what the sea was, but not yet what the water was.[15]

The goal of man and woman is to become the sea, to "get lost in Tao", to realize *tat tvam asi*, you are God or God is you. Whenever we read a text, we bring something to the text. Can we also read the Bible inter-textually, that is, in the light of Asian traditions? Where is the cutting edge in the different views of the human and of the divine? Is it not one of the difficulties of our world today that it seems as if there is nothing divine left in the world? God is the only one, and God is beyond everything. There is no trace of God. Brought up with our creation story, we do not feel that the tree is divine and needs to give us permission before we may take its fruit. Could Asian views liberate us from an idea of transcendence that has made the world seem void of the presence of God? On the other hand, can the Jewish tradition of simultaneous distance and proximity between God and humanity keep alive a dynamic in which human beings must always run the risk of critique? Identification or difference? In Heschel's words:

> Who is man? A being in travail with God's dreams and designs, with God's dream of a world redeemed, of reconciliation of heaven and earth, of a mankind which is truly his image, reflecting his wisdom, justice and compassion. God's dream is not to be alone, to have mankind as a partner in the drama of continuous creation. [16]

NOTES

[1] Lewis John Eron, "The Problem of a Jew Talking to a Christian about Jesus", in L. Swidler, ed., *Bursting the Bonds? A Jewish-Christian Dialogue on Jesus and Paul*, Maryknoll NY, Orbis, 1990, p.21.

[2] "Our Theological Task, VIII: Scriptures and Creeds", *The Guardian* (Madras), vol. XXV, no. 8, 20 Feb. 1947, pp.7f.

[3] "Christianity and Hinduism", *NCCR*, March 1928, p.128.

[4] *Ibid.*, p.135.

[5] *Ibid.*, p.138.

[6] "Our Theological Task", *loc. cit.*

[7] *Ibid.*

[8] Stanley S. Samartha, "The Asian Context: Sources and Trends", in R.S. Sugirtharajah, ed., *Voices from the Margin: Interpreting the Bible in the Third World*, London, SPCK, 1991, pp.46f.

[9] Israel Selvanayagam, "Jewish-Christian Relationship from a Third World Perspective", *Current Dialogue*, no. 25, 1993, p.21.

[10] *Ecumenical Considerations on Jewish-Christian Dialogue*, Geneva, WCC, 1983, p.9.

[11] UN Sub-Commission on Prevention of Discrimination and Protection of Minorities, cited in *Dictionary of the Ecumenical Movement*, Geneva, WCC, 1991, p.667.

[12] Leon Klenicki, "The Chosen People: A Contemporary Personal Jewish Perspective", presentation to the Consultation on the Church and the Jewish People (CCJP), Budapest, 15-21 October 1995.

[13] A.J. Heschel, *Who is Man?*, Stanford, Calif., Stanford U.P., 1965, p.5.

[14] Harold Kushner, *To Life!*, Boston, Little, Brown, 1993, p.59.

[15] Anthony Bloom, *Living Prayer*, London, Libra, 1966, pp.105f.

[16] Heschel, *op. cit.*, p.118.

I

The Experience
of Being a Minority

1. The Jewish Experience: Ghetto, Assimilation or...

ROBERT M. SELTZER

For more than twenty-five hundred years, the Jews have been a minority in many lands, east and west. Although the Jews were a majority in parts of the land of Israel until at least the third century CE, a Jewish diaspora has been in existence since the Babylonian exile of 586 BCE (some date its inception from the Assyrian conquest of the northern kingdom). At the beginning of the first century CE "there were devout Jews from every nation under heaven living in Jerusalem... Parthians, Medes, Elamites, and residents of Mesopotamia, Judaea, Cappadocia, Pontus and Asia, Phrygia and Pamphylia, Egypt and the parts of Libya belonging to Cyrene, and visitors from Rome, both Jews and proselytes, Cretans and Arabs..." (Acts 2:5-11). Josephus quotes the Greek geographer Strabo to the effect that there was hardly any place in the inhabited world without the presence of the Jews. [1]

By the Middle Ages there were branches of the diaspora in the Atlas mountains of Morocco, the highlands of Yemen and Ethiopia, the Eurasian steppes (Kievan Rus, the kingdom of the Khazars), the cities of central Asia (Samarkand, Bukhara), the Malabar coast (Cochin and other west Indian towns), China (Kaifeng) and perhaps other far-flung locations that have left no historical record. In modern times there is no region on any continent in the Old or New World that has not witnessed a flourishing Jewish community.

The meaning of "minority"

Before offering, as an historian of the Jews and Judaism, some generalizations on this extensive Jewish experience as a minority, I will make several conceptual or methodological observations.

First, the historical and sociological typology of a "minority" is not sufficiently nuanced to throw into relief what is unique about the Jewish case: that the Jews are followers of a religious tradition and members of a people, and that the two dimensions are umbilically tied. (To be sure, there are other groups which are both a distinctive religion and a people: the Sikhs in India, the Mormons in Utah, perhaps some of the national forms of Christianity such as the Armenians and the Ethiopians.) Moreover, the term "ethnicity" does not exactly apply to the Jews if "ethnic" is taken to mean particularism with no reference to universalism. There have been a number of distinct Jewish cultures in history: Hellenistic and Babylonian Judaism in antiquity, Arabic-speaking Jewries of the Middle East, the Judaeo-Persian subculture, which gave rise to many of the Jewries of Central and East Asia, the Italian Jewish tradition, which endured since the early Middle Ages, Ashkenazic Judaism, which appeared in northern France and western Germany in the early Middle Ages and spread to Eastern Europe, Sephardic Judaism, which arose in the Iberian penin- sula and was transplanted around the Mediterranean and the North Atlantic. But what maintained the overall unity under which these parts were subsumed was religious and not ethnic.

Second, the term "minority", as used by sociologists in the US at least, has come to mean a subordinate group, one "differentiated from others in the same society by race, nationality, religion or language". The entry on "minorities" in the *International Encyclopedia of the Social Sciences*, from which this definition comes, goes on to state that the members of a minority "both think of themselves as a differentiated group and are thought of by the others as a differentiated group with negative connotations. Further, they are relatively lacking in power and hence are subjected to certain exclusions, discrimina- tions and other differential treatment." Among the examples cited are the Jewish communities of Europe and Asia until recent decades. One wonders how this conception applies to the Christian situation in Asia, especially after the retreat of European imperialism in that part of the globe.

Third, I shall approach the topic schematically by differentiating the "pre-modern" from the "modern" Jewish experience as a minority. "Modernity" is very difficult to define, despite the considerable literature attempting to do so, because its essential features appear quite different from period to period and land to land. At the very least, "modernity" refers to a long series of drastic changes in society, culture and politics that began to appear in the seventeenth and eighteenth centuries, including a greatly increased secular sphere of life, a heightened sense of individual autonomy over against traditional religious imperatives, the ascendancy of scientific and pragmatic modes of treating problems and conceptions of sovereignty grounded in the whole people rather than in an aristocratic elite or a divinely authorized monarch. Whatever "modernity" will turn out to have been when it has finally given way to "post-modernity", it is considerably easier to distinguish modern from what preceded it — at least in Jewish history. I will therefore compare and contrast the "pre-modern" Jewish experience from the "modern" with respect to three crucial areas: community, persecution and self-identity.

Forms of Jewish community

With due regard for the wide range of Jewish social forms and institutions that are found through the twenty-five or more centuries of diaspora life, the Jewish community has always been a semi-autonomous collectivity embedded in a larger society divided into distinct estates or some comparable set of units. The structure of this larger society specified different rights and duties for each of these units. The liberties and limitations defining the status of the Jews differed from land to land and era to era, but Jews were almost always confined to certain economic niches, were excluded from the power elite (which was usually military in nature), had their own courts to handle disputes according to Jewish law and were granted the freedom to practise their religion as they saw fit.

Before the US Constitution of 1789, all countries in which Jews lived had had a state religion which thoroughly permeated society. Obviously, if Jews were not specifically allowed to worship in their own way, rear their children in their own religious tradition, observe the laws of *kashrut*, bury their dead according to Jewish practice and so forth, they simply could not live in that place. It should be noted that laws about such things as transfer of property and contracts posed no such problem because of the talmudic dictum *dina demalkhuta dina* — "the law of the kingdom is the law". In some domains there were conditions that applied only to the Jews: special taxes, limitations on the number that could marry, severe restrictions on engaging in many businesses and professions or owning land. In some places a ghetto was imposed on them (the word probably derives from the name of the iron-foundry district in 16th-century Venice where Jews were confined), but by and large the *Judengasse* or Jewish districts or Jew Towns (such as in Cochin) were places where Jews preferred to live in proximity to their religious institutions and each other.

Three corollaries need be mentioned. First, all pre-modern societies were characterized by some form of distinct segmentation, such as the division into citizens, slaves and resident aliens of classical Greece, the aristocracy, clergy, bourgeoisie and peasantry of *ancien regime* Europe, the millets of the Ottoman empire, castes in India and so forth. There was no general category of "citizen" as such.

Second, the self-segregation of the kind typical of pre-modern Jewry did not prevent interaction, often quite close, with the surrounding population and culture. Jews spoke the vernacular language of their neighbours (or a Jewish dialect of it, such as Yiddish or Ladino). They took customs and symbols from their neighbours and reworked them to fit the Jewish religious context. Examples of this among Ashkenazic Jews include the *yorzeit* practice for remembering the anniversary of the death of a parent, *yizkor* prayers in honour of the dead and the portable *huppa* bridal canopy under which a Jewish wedding was solemnized; more generally one may cite the six-pointed *magen David* (star of David), the architecture of synagogues and the shape and form of amulets. Pre-modern Jewish intellectual history shows many important links to the high and popular cultures of its environment, ranging from the influence of Plato on Philo of Alexandria to that of Alfarabi on Moses Maimonides, from the impact of the neo-Platonists on the Kabbalah to that of the Franciscan system of penances on the *Hasidei Ashkenaz*, the Jewish mystics of post-Crusades Europe.

The third corollary is that a religious or ethnic minority sometimes develops special skills, perhaps making use of their bonds to co-religionists in other lands, perhaps because their tradition inculcates a high degree of literacy, self-examination and deferred gratification. Especially in northern and eastern Europe, the Jews became such a distinctive socio-economic group; as historical parallels one may cite the Armenians, the Russian Old Believers and the Chinese in certain countries of southeast Asia, who developed significant diasporas and carved out a conspicuous role for themselves as economic inter-mediaries.

The modern Jewish community, which gradually took shape in Western Europe and North America in the 18th century, in Central Europe during the 19th century, and in Eastern Europe and elsewhere in the 20th century, was a response to a new political situation created by the absolutist state and, after the era of the French Revolution, by the nation-state. Based on quite different conceptions of the relation of government to citizen, the nation-state demolished the pre-modern estates and other internal social divisions as legal entities, erasing the privileges and disabilities attached to each of them. In theory every citizen was equal before the law — though of course there was a considerable gap between theory and practice. In Jewish history this process came be called, in the 1820s, "emancipation". The pre-modern semi-autonomous Jewish community was abolished: Jews no longer paid their taxes as a group but as individuals, and Jewish courts lost their authority. Gradually, Jews developed new forms of organi-zation (consistories, *gemeinde*, philanthropic bodies such as the *Alliance Française Universelle*, the British Board of Deputies, the Jewish Welfare Board). New channels of communication were created using such modern media as newspapers, journals and radio. In the West the Jewish community as a completely voluntary institution predominated. For well-known historical reasons this did not happen in the East, where other models of modern Jewish communal life were proposed, including multi-national states in which the cultural and other rights of ethnic and religious minorities, like the Jews, were to be constitutionally guaranteed. At the Versailles Peace Conference after the first world war, the successor-states to Austria-Hungary and Czarist Russia were forced to sign treaties formally confirming the rights of their minorities, but this experiment did not enjoy much success in the period between the wars.

The most important new form of communal reintegration in modern Jewish history is of course the State of Israel. The Zionist movement was predicated on the principle that as long as the Jews remained everywhere a minority, they would be vulnerable to the forces of persecution and of loss of identity. Accepting the primacy of the nation-state, Zionism sought to create a Jewish equivalent, in which Jews could find a solution to the defencelessness of a modern minority against the pressures that a modern state and dominant majority can bring to bear. Furthermore, the State of Israel gave the Jews (specifically, the Jews of the State of Israel) a recognized voice in the international arena and a means of rescuing threatened branches of the diaspora — thousands of concentration camp survivors after the second world war, Jews in Arab countries after 1948, Jews of Argentina during the bad years there, Falashas in Ethiopia, refusniks in the USSR, etc. The challenge which the State of Israel poses to Judaism is that for the first time in centuries Jews find they are a majority with minorities under their control, but that subject is beyond the scope of this essay.

Persecution and assimilation

The second element in the historical experience of the Jews as a minority is an extraordinary vulnerability to persecution. History presents various instances of minorities attacked, with or without the instigation of the government, by other groups among whom they lived. Examples include Christians in the Roman empire before Constantine and in Sassanian Persia before Islam, Jews and Christians in the Iberian peninsula under the Almoravides and, a century later, the Almohades, Jews and Muslims in Christian Spain after the unification of Castile and Aragon. In pre-modern times the Jews were the archetypal minority virtually unable to defend itself effectively against military or paramilitary forces. Some of these events became part of Jewish sacred history: the massacres in the Rhineland at the beginning of the First Crusade (1095), in many parts of Europe during the Black Death (1348-49), the anti-Jewish riots in Aragon and Castile in 1391, massacres in the Polish Ukraine by Bogdan Chmielnicki's Cossacks and local peasants (1648-49). Other dates recall the cruel expulsion of the Jews from lands where they had lived for centuries: England (1290), France (1394), Spain (1492), Portugal (1497). Incidentally, the only time the Jews of Cochin and nearby towns were persecuted was during the period of Portuguese rule.

Important as this aspect of Jewish history is, such massacres and expulsions were by and large punctuation marks during long stretches when Jews enjoyed a modicum of tranquillity and even relative prosperity. We will return later to the meaningfulness of Jewish suffering in pre-modern times, but one should also recall the periods during which Jews were invited to settle in certain Christian lands where they mixed peacefully with their neighbours, the eras when Jews borrowed extensively from the popular and high civilizations in their environment and in return contributed to them.

The dissolution of the old regimes under the impact of the great modern revolutions offered dramatic new opportunities for minorities previously excluded from the mainstream. The main intellectual force that shaped the new political order in Europe and the United States was the Enlightenment of the 18th century and its continuation in 19th-century liberalism. The Jews were not emancipated by a movement specifically directed to them alone; on the contrary, they were held to deserve equal rights before the law because they were subsumed under the most universal category of human beings as such. Emancipation, as we have seen, abolished traditional communal patterns and would pose an exacting challenge to Jewish philosophies and ideologies. But together with the economic transformations of modern times it opened up new ways of earning a living and acquiring an education and created a new sense of human dignity and self-worth. The great achievement of the modern revolution in human consciousness has been to awaken in individuals, ethnic and national groups, genders, castes and other subjugated sectors of society aspirations for realistic betterment, the right to be treated with courtesy and respect and the opportunity to be recognized in their particularity as part of universal humankind. Globally, Jews were one of the earliest of such particular groups to undergo the transition from the old to the new context of liberation and enfranchisement.

Regarding persecution of minorities, the Jewish experience shows that modern persecutions can be even more destructive than pre-modern ones. There is a much more devastating technology to use against the victims, more effective media for inflaming hatred, new devices and arrangements that can be harnessed, ranging from railroads to machine guns to concentration camps to poison gas chambers.

Ironies abound in the history of Jewish persecutions. The rationale for pre-modern persecutions was usually religious, but historians often detect economic and political reasons that made persecution tempting and convenient: to confiscate the wealth of Jews, to eliminate economic competitors or sometimes because the Jewish community had backed the wrong side in a power struggle. In modern persecutions the rationale has often been political and economic: Jews had too much power, they were arrogant and dominating, there was no defence but to attack them. What can be more useful than singling out a minority to blame, giving the illusion of doing something for the insulted and injured without rearranging the very mechanisms of exploitation that brought about the oppression? Under such secular arguments, however, lie irrational Manichean or apocalyptic motives that, for all their pseudo-scientific (racial or class-struggle) terminology, are often fundamentally quasi-religious.

A second dilemma that the modern Jewish minority has faced as a collectivity is the obverse of persecution: the loss of members through assimilation. The creation of a so-called "neutral society" (the term is used by social historian Jacob Katz for a zone neutral to specific religious identity) made it far easier for individual Jews to pull away from the Jewish community and eventually be absorbed into the majority. This is a concern because there are so few Jews — perhaps 12 million in the world. To be sure, Jews have always been a *she'erit ha-peletah*, a "remnant that escaped" (1 Chronicles 4:43). Although the vast majority of Jews are Jews by birth, there has always been a fluctuating stream of converts to Judaism ("Jews by choice" in the current terminology). In Europe and the United States today, where it is easy for Jews to assimilate, Jews increasingly resemble "Jews by choice" because, whether born as Jews or converts, they voluntarily choose to take their Jewish faith seriously and actualize it in their lives. This leads directly to our third theme, self-definition.

Uniqueness and identity

In pre-modern Judaism, Jews were a minority in fact but not in their own eyes. "Minority" is a numerical concept, not a spiritual one. While the traditional Christian replacement-theology held that the Old Israel, the Jewish people, was superseded by a New Israel, the church, Jews continued to view themselves as God's beloved, a people chosen by the Eternal in order to give his Torah a dwelling-place in human history. To quote the Labour Zionist intellectual Hayim Greenberg:

Until recent times we were, fundamentally, not a minority. We were a minority statistically only, but not psychologically. A soloist in a large philharmonic orchestra is not a minority of one among scores of other musicians. The early Christians who were persecuted in pagan Rome were not a minority in the sense in which we should understand this term. The Quakers in England 300 years ago were spiritually not a minority, though numerically they were insignificant... Jews survived as a numerical and persecuted minority in an alien world not because they were a separate tribe, a distinct people (in the modern, nationalist sense) or a different race. Tribes, peoples, racial groups disappeared many times when they mingled with others more numerous and stronger than they. The world cemetery is filled with the graves of such dead entities.

We were... something else: an exclusive group of believers, the Congregation of Israel. This is much more than a group sharing common memories (time and environment frequently eradicate group memories and eliminate them as influencing factors); it is more than blood kinship... During many centuries Jews were aware that, in addition to being a people like any other, a collective physical entity, they were also... a group of "conspirators" against the forces of darkness and uncleanness in the world, and that this "conspiracy" was part of Providence's plan leading to the "end of days" which would come about sooner or later — time was not a factor and it was not desirable to hasten the end. [2]

Jews were called to live according to God's revealed truth, the Torah. They were the people who assumed the "yoke of the commandments" and the privilege of demonstrating to God that they were obedient to the covenant into which their ancestors entered at Mount Sinai. There was a range of theological explanations for the persecutions Jews were forced to undergo from the time of Antiochus Epiphanes and Hadrian to the First Crusade and Chmielnicki's Cossacks, inasmuch as they could not be explained as punishment for any sin. They were a recapitulation of the *Akedah* ("binding of Isaac") of Genesis 22; they were *yisurin shel ahavah* ("chastisements of love") from a God who cared for them; they were a witness of the faithfulness of the people of Israel to the God it loved, and so forth. But these persecutions seldom ruptured Jewish faith and often strengthened it.

Modern Jewish theology has of course attempted to reinterpret and refine the meaning of the uniqueness of the people of Israel in line with the new intellectual assumptions and methodologies of the last few centuries: to explain in novel terms the continuities of Judaism, the mission of the Jewish people, the collective Jewish encounter with divinity. The greatest difference modernity brought was the realization on the part of the Jews that they were a "minority". They became fully aware of the impact Jews and Judaism have had on human history, but also of how feared, despised and hated they were and how helpless they could be when attacked.

As we have seen, modern Jews did try to defend themselves by creating new communal agencies and structures. These were of some value when there was still a modicum of the civilized conscience of humanity afoot, but they had no effect when confronted by the Nazis and their allies. The Holocaust intensified immensely the Jewish sense of powerlessness, indicating to the generation following the second world war that when the chips were down, there were few friends the Jews could count on (although to be sure there were some). Modern minorities are much more vulnerable, both physically and psychologically, to persecution, inasmuch as they have come to think that they have human rights. Perhaps the greatest ignominy is to be stripped of these rights in an attempt to force them back into subordinate status — or, even worse, to dehumanize them. Certainly one of the motives for Jewish efforts to memorialize the Holocaust is to exorcise the anger and guilt brought on by feelings of powerlessness resulting from it, as well as to derive some lessons about self-protection in the future.

We should, however, remember the positive features of modernity for minority self-identity, especially how modern historical consciousness enables a group to gain a more complete and nuanced comprehension of its heritage against the background of the whole of world history. At its best, modern historical consciousness broadens our sympathetic imagination, makes possible a deeper appreciation of bonds with other peoples and encourages the discovery of similarities between one's own tradition and the full panoply of human religious experience.

* * *

The subtitle of this essay — "Ghetto, Assimilation, or..." — correctly ends with an ellipsis. There are more options than either self-segregation in a pre-modern or modern ghetto or assimilation. Modern self-definition can entail a fruitful duality, in which a tradition is aware of itself both as a particularity and as part of a much larger whole, an awareness that can and should spill over into appropriate religious action. Thus, in pre-modern times there was little the Jews could do as a subjugated minority to further *tikkun ha-olam* ("repair of the world"). In modern times there are more opportunities and fewer excuses.

The new modern self-definition should result in spiritual enrichment, because by grasping the texture and symbolism of other faiths one comes to know one's own better. Insight into the other can help us to perceive elements which are potentially present in our own tradition but forgotten, obscured or eclipsed due to temporary conditions. For example, within Jewish mysticism there are versions of the spiritual life that are similar to south or east Asian religiosity. Christians in Asia, inasmuch as they now find themselves encountering Asian religions firsthand, without the prestige and power of European imperialism behind them, may be led to create new theological syntheses and to understand in this context more deeply what is distinctive about their Christianity.

Inasmuch as Judaism and Christianity have a special relationship, Jews should share in this undertaking of drawing biblical and post-biblical faith to a further degree of concrete universality. Jews and Asian Christians are both minorities living in populations many times larger. Productive dialogue may come from engaging in a common search, so that our two traditions may gain in knowledge, wisdom and mutual understanding.

NOTES

[1] Josephus, *Antiquities*, XIV. 115.
[2] Hayim Greenberg, *The Inner Eye*, II, 65f.

2. *Christians in Taiwan: Oppressed Majority and Alienated Minority*

HUANG PO HO

The working definition of "minority" by the United Nations sub-commission on prevention of discrimination and protection of minorities (cited in Hans Ucko's essay, p.xviii above), while acknowledging the numerical dimension, rightly identifies the function of power as a key to understanding the term "minority". This emphasis serves as an important clue for analyzing what it means for Christians to be a minority in Asian countries.

At a recent conference of the Programme of Theology and Culture in Asia (PTCA), under the theme "Doing Theology with Asian Resources", it was suggested that, besides the biblical stories, we need all kinds of stories of Asian people, especially folk stories, in order to reconstruct Christian theology in an Asian setting. In that story-telling spirit, I shall begin this essay by telling a story about a community of people with a hyphenated identity — namely, Asian-Christian — particularly from a Taiwanese experience. Since it is a story from a people with a complex identity, it has two aspects: a cultural-political *Asian* aspect and a religious *Christian* aspect. Through telling this story I hope to examine and briefly reflect on the real meaning of Christians as a minority in Asia.

Being Taiwanese: an oppressed majority
Taiwan is also known as Formosa, meaning "beautiful island" — the name given by Portuguese explorers in the 16th century. It lies about 160 kilometres off the southeast coast of China, from where the ancestors of many of its inhabitants originally came. This small, leaf-shaped island is the second most densely populated country in the world today. Most of Taiwan's 21 million people live in the cities and villages of the plains and foothills, largely on the west side of the

island. About 340,000 (less than 2 percent) are aborigines, who are divided into ten tribes. Racially and linguistically they are related to the Malayo-Polynesian people.

The largest segment of the population, often called "Taiwanese", makes up about 17 million, or 85 percent (75 percent Amoy-speaking, 10 percent Hakka-speaking). They are descendants of settlers from southeast China who began emigrating to Taiwan about four centuries ago to escape hardship and to seek freedom and happiness. At no time did these settlers come to Taiwan with the idea of contributing to the territorial expansion of China.

From the 17th century on, however, a succession of foreign governments (Portuguese, Dutch, Spanish and Manchu) took control of various parts of Taiwan. In 1887 the declining Ching Dynasty made Taiwan a province of China, but eight years later in 1895, when China lost the first Sino-Japanese war, Taiwan was handed over to Japan "in perpetuity". However, when Taiwan had been a Japanese colony for only 50 years, at the end of the second world war in 1945, the Allied powers instructed the Chinese Nationalist government to accept the Japanese surrender of Taiwan and to undertake, temporarily, the military occupation of the island as a trustee on their behalf.

In 1949, when China fell to Communist forces, the Nationalist government, along with many soldiers and civilians, fled to Taiwan; and so the people of Taiwan were once again under the rule of outsiders who are, numerically, an absolute minority.

Thus except for the brief interlude from 1945 to 1949, Taiwan has been effectively separated from mainland China since 1895. Because of this historical separation, Taiwan and China have developed along separate lines, resulting in quite different political, economic and cultural conditions. Therefore, despite the dream of the Nationalist government in Taiwan and its rival Communist government in Beijing — that Taiwan must belong to China — it is in fact neither necessary nor desirable to try to unite them. The "one-China policy" has been used by the ruling authority in Taiwan to refuse democratic political reform in Taiwan for the past decades. It is these factors which lead the Presbyterian Church in Taiwan, like many others, to prefer the "independence" option, supporting the right of self-determination for the people in Taiwan — to choose their own future without outside interference.

Taiwanese Christians: a creative but alienated minority

Since Christians are a minority in Taiwan, their position is just opposite to that of being Taiwanese, as we have introduced it above. The ironic situation in which a majority has been oppressed and a minority appears to be militant but alienated — and both of these identities are combined in the one person — characterizes the Christian role as a minority in Asia. In what follows I will take the Presbyterian Church in Taiwan (PCT) as an illustration of this irony.

Although Christianity came to Taiwan somewhat earlier with the arrival of Roman Catholic missionaries, Protestant mission work began with a missionary from the Presbyterian Church in England in 1865. From these early efforts, a Presbyterian church began to take shape in Taiwan. Because little modern development had been initiated by the government until the Japanese takeover in 1895, many modern institutions were first introduced to Taiwan by the church — the first school, the first hospital and the first printing press among others.

Since the second world war, Taiwan has been inundated with every variety of Christian mission, but among Protestant churches the PCT remains by far the largest, even though compared to the total population of Taiwan it is an absolute minority: only 4 percent of the population are Christians, and only 1 percent are Presbyterians. Yet despite being a small minority, the PCT has maintained a strong sense of social concern for the people of Taiwan and the future of the island. In the 1970s the church made three important proclamations: (1) a "Public Statement on Our National Fate" (1971); (2) "Our Appeal" (1975); and (3) a declaration on human rights (1977). These proclamations consistently emphasized the people's right of self-determination and a preference for the option of "independence".

Over the years, several Presbyterians have been among Taiwanese imprisoned for the peaceful expression of their ideas. But the PCT continues to identify with this island, to share the struggle of people and to be in solidarity with them. Yet in addition to this strong social concern and political involvement, in which the minority PCT has demonstrated its strong and positive attitude towards the fate of the people and the future of Taiwan, there is another aspect of the mission of the church which shows that a minority group can be very much militant and oppressive.

Christian missions in Asia, no matter from which denomination or missionary society, have come largely from Western civilizations which considered themselves "superior" and have thus been accompanied by an imperialist colonial mentality. An exclusive attitude towards the traditional religions and cultures of Asia has been taken by Christian churches of almost all confessions in this region. This has led to a misunderstanding of Christian mission as a technique of converting people from other faiths; and this misunderstanding has resulted in a desire to destroy the traditional religions and to degrade native cultures. Even the PCT, a church that claims to have strong identification with the people, has not been able to avoid this problem. Several churches, especially some of those that came from China after 1945 with the defeated KMT (the Nationalist Party in Taiwan), have even sided consistently with the power structures to exploit and oppress the people.

What does it mean to be a minority?

Reading these stories, we are immediately confronted by the question of what "minority" really means in an Asian context. How does the UN definition of minorities mentioned earlier apply to the situation in this region? Based on an analysis of the above stories, I have some observations and reflections:

(1) As Taiwanese Christians — an ethnic majority but a religious minority — our feelings and experiences are complex. On the one hand, as a majority "Taiwanese people" we have both oppressed the aboriginal minority through social domination, cultural discrimination and economic exploitation, and have been oppressed by a succession of alien minority groups from outside who have been our political rulers. On the other hand, as members of a Christian community we have been an absolute minority in the midst of a religiously pluralistic Asian society. We have encountered two aspects of being a religious minority. First, we have faced the reality of being excluded (as a reaction to our exclusive understanding of mission), discriminated against, marginalized from the society, in some places even threatened with death. But second, by struggling as a minority, the Christian churches in Asia have also found an opportunity to use their dynamics and creativity to make a contribution to their people and society.

(2) Christians, although a minority in all Asian countries except the Philippines, are not merely a weak minority in their societies. They can be a creative and powerful minority in either constructive or destructive ways in the societies where they find themselves.

(3) It is very important for Asian Christian churches to arrive at a self-understanding of their identity as creative minority and to come to see their mission as the mission of God (*missio Dei*) rather than the mission of the church. A re-examination of Christian identity and the meaning of mission can provide a new setting for churches in this region to reclaim their roles as partners in and contributors to Asian societies. Based on this perspective of Christian identity, churches in this region will be able to act as a prophetic community, and work for their own salvation (from the distortion of being a church) as well as that of other minority groups. Nevertheless, they are also called to work for the powerless, no matter whether they are a minority or a majority, where their humanity and dignity are in danger of being exploited — the liberation task.

Based on the above analysis and reflection on the stories, we can say that the minority experience, from an Asian perspective, has not only to do with the reality of being small and weak in the numerical sense. There is also another dimension: the qualitative sense of suffering and being oppressed by those in power. This means that the term "minority" becomes a problem, mainly because the function of power has produced injustice and an oppressive condition or atmosphere against the powerless, especially minorities.

Identity depends on one's relation to others. A minority feeling, therefore, means a problem of relationship. So in order to resolve the problem of being a minority, we must first confront our relationship with the people around us. Christians as a minority in Asia must search for a relevant self-understanding of their identity and seek to build up a healthy relationship with their neighbours, so that they can contribute to others from whom they claim to have been called out by God as a "divine community".

The minority complex created a fear of losing self-identity. This in turn led to an attitude of doing mission in an exclusive way, a refusal of dialogue with people of other faiths and an obsession with expanding the community by a kind of militant evangelistic approach. These attitudes should be re-examined and these energies re-directed.

3. How the Protestant Church Has Won the Chinese People

CHENFANG LO

When I say that the church has won the Chinese people, I do not mean that most Chinese people have become Christians. Christians are still a minority among the Chinese people, but through the vicissitudes of the past 150 years the Protestant church has become open to the Chinese people and many have found their spiritual needs satisfied there.

A brief historical survey

Protestant Christianity was introduced into China under the protection of foreign powers after the Opium War of 1840. The Chinese people thus regarded Christianity as a foreign religion, and they hated Christians, whom they saw as friends of the foreign aggressors. In 1922 an anti-Christian movement was launched among Chinese intellectuals: churches were attacked and church workers molested. After that a group of enlightened Christian leaders launched a movement to build an indigenous church which would be independent of foreign missionaries. That movement was later known as the Three-Self Movement — self-governing, self-supporting and self-propagating.

Since the church was in the hands of foreign missionaries, the Three-Self Movement did not at first meet with much success, although both Chinese Christians and foreign missionaries agreed with its principles. It was only after the liberation of 1949, the year in which the People's Republic of China was founded, that the Three-Self Movement began to gain momentum. In the light of the socialist revolution, Chinese Christians began to discover in the Bible the truths they had ignored. Formerly estranged from their own people through their adherence to a foreign religion, Chinese Christians now saw in the Old Testament that the patriarchs and prophets had a deep consciousness of patriotism. Recognizing that they should return to the embrace of the Chinese people, they launched accusations against some church leaders who were opposed to the Chinese revolution, which had made war on foreign aggressors and feudal landlords.

From 1951 to 1956 Chinese church workers underwent the self-education of patriotism. From study of the modern history of China, they saw how the backwardness of China was caused by foreign aggression and oppression and how the martyrs of the Chinese revolution had won freedom and independence for the Chinese people at the cost of their lives, like Old Testament prophets such as Moses and others who were willing to die for their people. But Chinese Christians also realized that they had made no contribution to the founding of the People's Republic. In the early days of the People's Republic, when the Chinese people expressed their joy on their National Day, the reaction of Christians recalled what Jesus once said about the children "sitting in the market place and calling to one another, 'We played the flute for you, and you did not dance; we wailed, and you did not weep'" (Luke 7:32).

The Chinese people welcomed Christians returning to the embrace of the people. Church leaders became people's representatives at all levels, from deputies in the National People's Congress to representatives in district people's congresses. During the ten years of the Great Cultural Revolution, when the Chinese people suffered Chinese Christians suffered with them. Thereafter the church emerged as an independent church, and Christianity is not now regarded as a foreign religion.

When all religions were suppressed during the Cultural Revolution, their leaders were forced to do manual labour, some of them labouring shoulder to shoulder on state farms. In their common life they began to understand one another. Leaders from various religions now meet regularly in people's congresses and people's political consultative conferences on different levels. They stand together in a common effort to win more and more religious liberty. A Muslim leader in Nanjing once told me that Muslims and Christians have more common ground with each other than with Buddhists because we both believe in one God; however, I have also discussed with a Buddhist friend how the self-negation Jesus taught his followers — that they should deny themselves — is a common goal for Buddhists and Christians, although by different means.

In the early 1950s the number of Chinese Protestant Christians was 700,000. The consequences of the Cultural Revolution decreased this number greatly, but during the past fifteen years, according to the most conservative statistics, the number has grown to seven million — nearly ten times more than in the first years after liberation. Over the past five years more than six million Bibles have been printed in China, but there is still an ever-increasing demand for Bibles all over the country. There is a deep reverence for the Bible even among non-Christians in China. In Nanjing some medical students who are not Christians formed a Bible study group. They learned from the Bible the teaching of Jesus that one should forgive others seventy times seven. A group of non-Christian scholars preparing a new translation of the Bible for Chinese intellectuals has asked professors from Nanjing Union Theological College to revise their translation. Since books on Christianity are best-sellers in China, some non-Christian scholars have written books on Christianity and the Bible, including a Bible dictionary which has been reprinted many times.

The image of God and the people of God

"God's image" may be defined as the inherent dignity or worth of a human being on account of his or her wisdom or reason. When we say that the human person is created in God's image, we emphasize not only his or her intrinsic value but also creatureliness. God's image also signifies the life of the first man and woman in Paradise — their happiness, innocent obedience to God and fellowship with God. The warning in Genesis that "whoever sheds the blood of a human, by a human shall that person's blood be shed; for in his own image God made humankind" (9:6) is a further assertion of the inherent dignity or worth of the human person. A passage with similar overtones is found in the New Testament letter of James: "With the tongue we bless the Lord and Father, and with it we curse those who are made in the likeness of God" (3:9).

In ancient China the famous Confucianist Mencius asserted that human nature is good. He said, "Everybody naturally has sympathy. Everybody has the sense of right and wrong. Everybody has the sense of shame and dislike." When orthodox Confucianists say that human nature is good, they are referring to the moral nature of the human person. But when some, for example Xunzi, say human nature is bad, they are putting this theory forward as the basis of a kind of political philosophy. In Christian language we may say that the characterization of human nature as good lays emphasis on the human condition before the fall, and to say that it is bad points to the condition after the fall. As humanists, Confucianists in general do not acknowledge the creatureliness of the human person.

The Old Testament says nothing about the divine image being lost; and the Priestly Code emphasizes that it was transmitted to Seth. Nevertheless, the steady decline of life-span from the long lives of the earliest patriarchs has the theological implication of a degeneration of the divine image. Protestant theologians have put forward the doctrine of total depravity, caused by human sin, which does not eradicate the divine image but causes it to malfunction. The human being is a moral animal, and morality presupposes responsibility. Responsibility depends on knowledge. Since the human creature is a rational or intellectual creature, he or she remains in the image of God even after the fall of Adam. The divine image may be diminished or even effaced by reason of sin. But this is not linked with the fall but with the individual sin of a specific person or groups of persons. A human person may be totally sinful; he or she is then not "materially" in the image of God (that is, in a right relationship with God). In the dimension of salvation, that is to say, in the dimension of the "material" image of God, a saving relationship with God can be established by God's grace, by faith alone.

In the Old Testament the people of God have a special covenant relationship with God and they are sanctified to be God's people (Exodus 19:4-7; Deuteronomy 7:6). In the New Testament this special relationship with God is realized through the blood of Christ, which is Christ's "blood of the new covenant" (Mark 14:24). Through this close relationship with Jesus, Christians can enter into this special relationship with God. Justification by faith is the basic teaching of the New Testament. We are justified before God not by observing the Old Testament law but by personal trust in Jesus.

In the Christian view only those who are justified by faith constitute the people of God. Paul said, "For not all Israelites truly belong to Israel, and not all of Abraham's children are his true descendants; but 'it is through Isaac that descendants shall be named for you'. This means that it is not the children of the flesh who are the children of God, but the children of the promise are created as descendants" (Romans 9:6-8). Christians are Abraham's spiritual descendants, as Paul said elsewhere: "if you belong to Christ, then you are Abraham's offspring, heirs according to the promise" (Galatians 3:29). When Paul said, "As for those who follow this rule — peace be upon them, and mercy, and upon the Israel of God" (Galatians 6:16), by "the Israel of God" he meant the Christian church. "This rule" means that those who are justified by faith will become God's new creation.

According to the Bible the people of God should renounce every kind of idolatry (Deuteronomy 4:23). This seems too uncompromising with regard to other religions. For example, if we trace the history of Buddhism in China, we see that Buddhism is very different from the Chinese culture, and there are contradictions between Buddhism and Confucianism. But the Chinese people are in need of religion, and Confucianism as a system of ethical teachings cannot meet their religious need. It is not necessary to change the doctrine of Buddhism to avoid offending the Confucianists. In cultural exchanges there may be contradictions, and the way to resolving them does not consist in compromise. The abiding truth of a religion will be assimilated by a different culture, just as Buddhism was assimilated by the Chinese culture. The best way of conducting dialogues between different religions is to speak and listen with an open and sympathetic mind.

God's choice of Israel was not a matter of favouritism. As the prophet Amos said, "Hear this word that the Lord has spoken against you, O people of Israel, against the whole family that I brought up out of the land of Egypt: 'You only have I known of all the families of the earth; therefore I will punish you for all your iniquities'" (Amos 3:1-2). To be the people of God is not only a privilege but also an obligation. Jesus said, "From everyone to whom much has been given, much will be required; and from the one to whom much has been entrusted, even more will be demanded" (Luke 12:48).

II

In God's Image

4. The Image of God in the Jewish Tradition

"*And God created the human being in God's image, in the image of God, God created humans, male and female God created them*" (Genesis 1:27).

Before we can discuss what it means to be created in the image of God, we have to ask the question — "What is God's image?" According to Jewish tradition, there are two aspects to the Divine: *the hidden* and *the manifest*. The hidden aspect of God is beyond human grasp, and whatever I shall say here thus relates to the manifest aspect of God.

What is God's image? According to one system of thought it is a combination of differing, sometimes conflicting attributes. On the one hand, God is the warrior: "The Lord is a warrior; the Lord is his name" (Exodus 15:3). On the other hand, he is the maker of peace (*shalom* in Hebrew). Or, as the book of Job puts them together: "Dominion and fear are with God; he makes peace in his high heaven" (25:2). *Shalom* is both a particular attribute and the name of the whole, which, as I said, is a combination of differing factors — heaven and earth, light and darkness, war and peace.

Jewish literature after the Hebrew Bible often takes the form of midrash, which is a combination of biblical interpretation, exegesis and narrative. This vast corpus of literary writings portrays a variety of opinions and a plurality of thought. One such midrash talks about the essence of God from a harmonizing point of view as a combination of complementary attributes: "There are seven qualities of God: wisdom, righteousness, justice, loving kindness, compassion, truth and peace." As it is written in the book of Hosea (2:21), "I will espouse you forever [= wisdom]. I will espouse you with *righteousness* and *justice* and with *loving care* and *compassion* and I will espouse you with *faithfulness*. Then you will be peace to God [or, more literally, then will you *know* the essence of God]".

Rabbi Meir asked: "What does it mean to know the essence of God — to know what Peace means?" And he answers: "When a human possesses these seven qualities, then that human truly understands God." These seven form the unit named *shalom*, meaning both peace and the whole.

Having said that *shalom* — the whole, the unity — is a making of peace between attributes, what then does it mean to be born in the image of God?

Rabbi Simeon, son of Halafta, said:

Peace is supreme, for when God created the world, God brought peace to the upper and lower spheres. On the first day of creation, God created from the upper spheres and the lower ones, as it is written in Genesis: "In the beginning God created the heaven and earth." On the second day God created from the upper spheres, as it is said: "Let there be an expanse." On the third day God created from the lower spheres, as it is said: "Let the water below be gathered." On the fourth day from the upper spheres — the lights. On the fifth day from the lower spheres — the living creatures of the sea. When on the sixth day God came to create the human being, God said: "If I create humans from the upper spheres then the upper spheres will have one extra creation, and if humans are created from the lower spheres then the lower spheres will have one extra creation. Therefore, humans will be created from both spheres" — as it is written — "God formed the human from the dust of the earth (lower spheres) and God blew into his nostrils the breath of life (upper spheres)", thus the creation of the human being keeps the harmony of creation.

In biblical Judaism the living creature is one integrated body and soul, but in Judaism after the Hebrew Bible, as in other thought systems of the Graeco-Roman period, the human being is seen as pulled between two conflicting drives: the spiritual and the carnal.

Six things can be said about human beings, according to the Talmud (*Hagiga* 17a). In three they are like the ministering angels: they have intellect, they walk upright and they can speak the holy tongue. In three they are like the beasts: they eat and drink, they procreate and they excrete their waste.

This doctrine of the two inclinations is a major feature of rabbinic psychology and anthropology. As a personification of the permanent dualism of the choice between good and evil, the rabbinic notion of the two inclinations shifts this dualism from a metaphysical to a more psychological level: tendencies in the human person rather than two cosmic principles. However, even the so-called *jetzer hara* (evil inclination), which corresponds roughly to untamed human natural (and especially sexual) appetites or passions, is not intrinsically evil. Therefore it cannot be completely suppressed, for without it a human being would never marry, beget children, build a house — in short, the world would not exist. It is only when it gets out of hand that it becomes the cause of harm.

How should the human being make peace between these opposing drives? For that the human being needs the guidance of the Torah.

A rabbinic midrash (*Shab*. 89) depicts the scene when Moses goes up to heaven to receive the Torah. Upset to see a mortal among them, the angels ask God why he is there. When God tells them that Moses came to get the Torah, they are upset that God's precious Torah, which God had preserved for 974 generations before creation, should now be given to human beings. God directs Moses to respond to them. Moses hears the contents of the Torah and asks the angels: "It is written, honour your father and your mother. Do you have fathers and mothers? It is written, you shall not murder. Are there murderers among you?"

The angels then realize that the Torah was especially created for human beings, for it is their ordering, guiding and disciplining principle and it is the means to approach the knowledge of God's essence. Study and observance of the Torah are an antidote to sin that crouches at the door. By creating the Torah especially for human beings, God has placed humankind above all creation. God has made the humans the crown of creation, master of the earth. By "master" God meant, I think, to make us responsible for keeping the cosmos in harmony, in peace, in a whole.

It is relevant, however, that the human was born last so that if he were to have too much pride, he could be reminded that the smallest insect was born before him (*Sanh*. 38).

Just as the creation of the world is a process of peacemaking between upper and lower spheres, so too the end of days, the final redemption, is seen in terms of cosmic and human harmony: "In the days to come... many nations shall come and say: 'Come, let us go up to the mountain of the Lord... God will judge between many peoples, and shall arbitrate between strong nations far away...; they shall all sit under their own vines and under their own fig trees... All the peoples walk, each in the names of its gods, but we will walk in the name of the Lord our God" (Micah 4:1-5).

Between these two poles — the beginning of time and the end of time — lies the human road. Taking the human road implies two major tasks, both arising from the human's purpose on earth: improving oneself (*tikkun atsmi*) and improving one's environment in the world (*tikkun olam*).

The human and the world, as we have learned by now, were created incomplete (not whole) on purpose. To be human means eternally to improve oneself and the world. By taking this task on our shoulders, we humans take part in the creation of the world. Since creation is a perpetual process — humanity and world being created anew every minute — sharing the godly creation means to be born in God's image. Jews set out to do this task through our world of *mitzvot*, each generation completing what the generation before did not complete. God has told us what is good and what the Lord requires of us: "to do justice, and to love kindness, and to walk humbly with your God" (Micah 6:8).

When we define the human being we bear in mind three principles: the unity of humankind, the equality of male and female and the individual value of each human being. I have not yet elaborated on one of those principles which is vital to me personally — and that is the fact that the term "Adam" (humankind) combines male and female.

Until modern liberal interpretation, Judaism has put the female factor in the shade: woman's labour lies within the home. As a law-centred religion, Judaism has exempted women from many commandments. However, the modern liberal streams of Judaism have come to reinterpret the story of creation as a starting point for regaining women's role as an essential part of what the whole human being means. Thus, Reform and Conservative Jewish women of today take on themselves by choice all commandments and share Jewish life in all its aspects.

5. *The Asian Struggle to Understand the Human*

S. WESLEY ARIARAJAH

What is the mystery of life and death — of being a human being in this world of names and forms?

The ancient song of the *Katha Upanishad* says that the wise know the secret which the ignorant will never understand:

> Fools, dwelling in the very midst of ignorance,
> but fancying themselves as wise and learned,
> go round to and fro, like the blind leading the blind.
> The truth of the hereafter does not shine
> before that childish person who is inattentive,
> and befooled by the delusion of wealth.
> "This world, seen by the senses *is, and there is no other*" —
> thinking thus, he falls into death's clutches
> again and again! (2.5-6).

And it goes on to set forth the basis of life as only the wise understand:

> The wise man knows that he is not born nor does he die;
> he has not come into being from anything;
> nor has anything come into being from him.
> This self of man is unborn, eternal,
> everlasting and ancient;
> it is not destroyed when the body is destroyed...
> Realizing the Atman as the bodiless in the bodies,
> the changeless in all changing entities,
> infinite and all-pervading,
> the wise does not grieve (2.18-20).

This basic wisdom about the unborn and the imperishable in every human life is only one of many streams of Indian thought that have struggled to understand humanity's place on the earth and in the universe. The religions of the original inhabitants of India, the thoughts and reflections of the waves of people who moved into the Indian mainland over the centuries and the interaction and amalgamation of these thoughts, aspirations and cultures have created a complex matrix of religious thought and action. Generally, Christians have looked on the religions of India — and of Asia as a whole — with a mixture of awe and suspicion, of deep respect and fear.

Nature and the human

Like the Psalmist and the sages of India, the Indian Christian agrees that it is "fools" who say in their hearts that there is no God (Psalm 14:1). But the story that controls the Indian Christian understanding of the relationship between humans, nature and God is the second account of creation in the book of Genesis: "Then the Lord God formed man from the dust of the ground, and breathed into his nostrils the breath of life; and the man became a living being..." (2:7). The conclusion of that story has also had its impact on the Indian Christian mind: "By the sweat of your face you shall eat bread until you return to the ground, for out of it you were taken; you are dust, and to dust you shall return" (3:19).

Despite the contemporary rereading of the Genesis stories to underscore human stewardship of and responsibility for nature, despite the recovery of the wisdom tradition within the Old Testament, which celebrates nature and its relationship to God in its own right, a substantial gap remains between the biblical approach and Asian religious traditions. The latter reflect a deep sense of kinship between the human and the non-human which leads them to look at nature from a relational, intuitive, mystical and aesthetic standpoint rather than from an analytical one.

The issue is not simply one of attitude. Behind the approach of Asian religions is an understanding of nature as a self-contained and self-ordered reality upheld by its own organizing principle (the Tao, the Dharma). Human life is only a part of this. Humans are neither above nature nor apart from it, but live in a reciprocal relationship to it and are governed by the very same principle that governs and sustains the universe. The Buddhist principle of dependent origination sees all life, including the human, as interdependent and interconnected: one cannot move a pebble on the seashore without reordering the whole universe. The Upanishads clearly insist that the Ultimate, the Real, the Eternal One (also called "God") pervades and fills the universe, standing with, alongside, under, above and in it: "The Supreme Being is moving and yet is still. He is near everybody yet is far away. He is immanent in all beings yet is external to them."

The text goes on to draw the consequence for all other relationships of seeing reality in this manner:

> The one who sees all creatures and matter in the Supreme Being
> and the Supreme Being in all creatures and matter
> bears no malice towards any being.
> When the enlightened attains the knowledge of Brahman,
> then he perceives the underlying unity
> and resemblance to himself of all creatures.
> Thus when he gains the insight that the one Divine Being
> is existent in all beings,
> then whom shall man love and whom shall he hate? (*Ishavasya* 1.5-7)

In their quest to understand what it means to be human, Asian Christians have struggled with this double heritage of biblical and Asian thought, with their two remarkably different approaches to humanity's relation to nature and the divine. In so doing, Asian Christians have been mindful that what seems at first glance to be a lofty view of the unity of all things has manifested some negative effects in Asian societies.

For the traditional Asian view that the "law" which maintains the harmony of nature also governs the life of individuals and society has often had dehumanizing and even demonic consequences. Rigid and oppressive social structures like the caste system and emperor worship have been justified as part of the social order required by the natural law. It was argued that this is part of the way in which the necessary diversity in society is knitted into a social harmony. And those who would not be accommodated within the system, like the dalits, become "outcastes". Within Confucianism and Shintoism the call not to violate the "ordering of nature" has been abused to maintain oppressive hierarchies and to exclude women from being true and equal partners in family and society.

Christians, whose scriptural tradition bears witness to a God who intervenes in history on behalf of the oppressed and marginalized, and who see their own mission as a prophetic ministry to change what must be changed, have had considerable difficulty relating to this element of their Asian heritage. Many Christians have seen such an understanding of the human as a static view which leads to fatalism and superstition and undermines the urgency "to do justice and to correct oppression" in the life of both individuals and society.

Yet in the contemporary debate on humanity and nature, Asian Christians have been unwilling to reject Asian wisdom on the relationship of God, humanity and nature as leading inevitably to superstition and oppression. Faced with the consequences of human alienation from nature in the ecological crisis, which is an increasingly serious issue in Asia, Asian Christian theologians are well aware of the dangers of viewing nature as something to be manipulated and of the inherent threat to human life when the sense of a wider community of life encompassing the whole creation is lost.

In the search for a Christian understanding, one of the directions, in Asia as elsewhere, has been to rediscover and re-own the closeness of nature and history attested to in several parts of the scripture, including those Psalms which celebrate creation as the manifestation of God's own beauty and faithfulness and the Pauline vision that creation itself "waits with eager longing" for its redemption and transformation in order to participate in the glory of the children of God (Romans 8:19ff.).

But the task goes deeper than a mere selective re-reading of scripture. Many Asian Christian thinkers would agree with Sri Lankan theologian Aloysius Pieris that the biblical and Asian views of the human and its relationship to nature are two poles, two approaches, two insights about reality that need and complement and correct each other. Either one without the other remains a partial view. Both approaches to nature and God are essential for a complete vision and understanding of the human.

Thus, a consultation on humanity and nature that brought together some leading Asian Christian theologians in Manila identified nine issues that have to be faced in the attempt to understand what it means to be human in the Asian context:

First, we need to ask whether there has been an over-emphasis on the transcendence or "otherness" of God over man and nature, and a qualified transcendence of man over nature... The Asian cultural emphasis on the immanence of the Holy, the self-sufficiency of nature and the need to have a reciprocal relation to nature must be taken seriously...

Second, what is the relationship of man to nature? Does the biblical image of responsible stewardship exhaust all that can be said about it? What does the relational understanding within the Asian faiths say about the way to relate man to nature?

Third, in what ways can we accelerate and participate in those processes that liberate man from demonic manifestations of "nature relationships"? How can we deal theologically with the dehumanizing and "de-naturalizing" effects of technology and modernization?

Fourth, how can we understand and evaluate the process of life in Asia today? There are many attempts to understand it primarily in terms of categories of history. Is it adequate and true to the Asian reality...?

Fifth, a purely linear understanding of time which is implied in the biblical tradition tends to absolutize a consecutive understanding of processes or events in history and nature. It also fails to recognize the positive values of seeing time in a seasonal sense, which implies hopes of repetitive opportunities. It may be helpful to explore ways in which these two experiences of time can be brought together for mutual correction and enrichment.

Sixth, there is a tendency in Christian theology to consider morality in terms of given codes of behaviour. Many Asian religions, with their understanding of nature, have developed a corpus of moral teachings. There is a theological need to relate these teachings to the biblical Wisdom traditions, which also speak of nature as a teacher.

Seventh, similarly in popular Christian understanding, man's alienation from God (sin) is seen as failure to obey. Some Asian traditions see this alienation in terms of man's relation to nature as well. What is the understanding of sin in a nature-oriented culture and what new dimensions does it open to the Christian concept of sin?

Eighth, the Asian orientation also raises basic questions about the way we understand salvation. On the one hand, the political realities of society are pressing us to reformulate the concept of salvation. Equally important are the questions raised by attitudes towards nature. Can the search in some religious traditions for a coherent relationship between God-man-fellowman and nature serve as a corrective to the individualistic, communalistic, legalistic and future-oriented outlook on salvation?

Ninth, what does the nature-man relation in Asia say about life-styles, concept of work, spirituality etc.?[1]

This list of issues points not so much to a specifically Asian Christian understanding of the relationship of the human to the divine and to nature as to an unease with the human-centred view of life and history that came to Asia with the Christian faith. Nevertheless, the participants in this consultation recognized that the theological programme outlined here for the Asian Christian churches would emerge only as Asian Christians immersed themselves more fully in the spiritual traditions and historical realities of Asia.

Humanity and humanization

If spirituality and the emphasis on the unity of life form one pole of the Asian reality that shapes an understanding of the human, the other pole consists of the crushing poverty, deprivation and dehumanization of the masses of people in Asia. Nearly all Asian Christian theologians agree that any reflection on the human in the Asian context must approach it from the perspective of human liberation.

In this area the Asian Christian understanding is deeply influenced by the first creation narrative in Genesis, which affirms that the human is created in the image and likeness of God. Even if the Protestant over-emphasis on the "fall" and depravity of human nature have clouded the dignity accorded to the human by this creation narrative, the Christian church has been able, at least in theory, to argue for the fundamental unity, equality and dignity of all human beings before God and one another.

The interpretation of the gospel and of the person and work of Christ as that which ushered in a "new humanity", and the understanding of the community of faith as the Body of Christ, a koinonia rooted ontologically in the reality of the risen Christ, have strengthened this radical teaching on the dignity and equality of all human beings. In many ways this provides a needed corrective to the hierarchical and often oppressive systems built on the unitive view of life. Whether the Christian church in Asia has itself escaped the traps of casteism, hierarchical ordering of its social expression and the secondary place offered to women is another question, which needs serious attention. But unlike in South Africa, where sections of the church sought theological justification for the system of apartheid, Christians in Asia have never compromised the message of the gospel as that which liberates the human from every form of bondage.

For the Asian Christian, therefore, to be human is to recover one's dignity as a human person, to be liberated from whatever spiritual, social or political forces hold one captive, to be enabled to enter a community in which there is true mutuality and shared life. True humanity in this sense should not only be affirmed in theological and conceptual categories expressing the freedom and dignity of the human person, male and female, but also realized in the basic right to life — materially, socially and politically.

For this reason such Asian theologians as M.M. Thomas have spoken of salvation as "humanization" and the gospel as that which enables one to become truly human, after the likeness of Christ. Thomas goes on to speak of the church as a "community of forgiven sinners" which is called to be "God's instrument of the permanent revolution". The centrality of humanization in his understanding of what is human is attested to by his conviction that whatever is liberating in the secular movements and indigenous religions of India is itself part of the *one* liberative activity of God. From this Thomas develops the idea of an "integral humanism" which is "spiritually informed by the insights of the prophetic Christian faith and by the humanism of Asia's indigenous religions and cultures". [2]

In this search for human dignity and liberation Asian Christian theology tries to hold together the emphasis on the human as part of nature with the emphasis on the human as a conscious historical being. Asian Christian thought has thus had difficulty with the understanding of "salvation history" that was imported into Asia, in which the focus is on the history of Israel, which then narrows down to the "Christ event" and then broadens once more, but only to the boundaries of the Christian church. In short, "salvation history" that excludes the history of most of humankind and is detached from the process of humanization of all societies cannot be a history in which God is involved.

This is why C.S. Song, for example, challenges the view of salvation history popularized by Oscar Cullmann. While rejecting the idea of salvation history as God's limited activity in the history of one nation and the church, Song is fascinated by the way in which Israel could read and discern God's guiding hand and purpose within its history, thus giving a salvific meaning to what might otherwise have been mere "secular" events. In other words, salvation history is history read with the eyes of faith; one discovers "salvation history" in making connections with the humanization processes in which God is involved in one's history.

On this understanding, Song has no difficulty perceiving the possibility of a salvific reading of the history of Asian societies:

> In the light of the experiences unique to Israel, other nations should learn how their histories can be interpreted redemptively. An Asian nation would have its own experiences of exodus, captivity, rebellion against heaven, the golden calf. It would have its own long trek in the desert of poverty or dehumanization. What a nation goes through begins to take a redemptive meaning against the background of the history of Israel, symbolically transported out of its original context to a foreign one. An Asian nation will thus be enabled to find its place side by side with Israel in God's salvation.[3]

To ask whether such a redemptive reading of Asian histories is appropriate and required is not, of course, our intention here. But it is important to realize that both M.M. Thomas and C.S. Song are after the same thing: to give historical rootedness to the understanding of what is human in Asian Christian understanding.

One might say that the Asian Christian search to understand the human and its destiny is fed by three streams: (1) Asian spiritual, cultural and scriptural traditions; (2) the Jewish-Christian tradition of the Bible; and (3) the actual historical realities of Asian societies. The meeting of these three streams has not been easy because of the deep diversity of what we have been referring to in general terms as Asian spirituality and culture, considerable disagreement among Christians over how to read and interpret the Bible and the profound changes that have taken and are taking place in the histories of Asian nations.

Pointing to the rapid social, political and cultural changes that have come to characterize all Asian societies, an Asian theologian once said that "in Asia, one has to do theology on the run!" That so many Asian theologians today are in fact willing to do "theology on the run" — to participate in this long and difficult marathon — is itself a sign of hope.

NOTES

[1] Emerito P. Nacpil and Douglas J. Elwood, *The Human and the Holy: Asian Perspectives in Christian Theology*, Manila, New Day Publishers, 1978, pp.67-69.
[2] M.M. Thomas, "Christian Action in the Asian Struggle", in Douglas J. Elwood, ed., *What Asian Christians are Thinking*, Manila, New Day Publishers, 1976, pp.450f.
[3] C.S. Song, "From Israel to Asia — A Theological Leap", in *Theology*, March 1976, pp.90-96.

6. Asian Realities: Oppression and Dehumanization

WONG WAI CHING ANGELA

After recording that "God created humankind in his image, in the image of God he created them; male and female he created them..." (Genesis 1:27), the book of Genesis says that God assigned human beings stewardship over the earth and its living creatures. This reference to creation in the image of God is repeated in chapter 5:1-2: "When God created humankind, he made them in the likeness of God. Male and female he created them and he blessed them." In Psalm 8:4-5, we read: "What are human beings that you are mindful of them, mortals that you care for them? Yet you have made them a little lower than God, and crowned them with glory and honour." From Colossians 1:15 we learn that Christ also shares, in a way, this same image of God with us, for "he is the image of the invisible God, the firstborn of all creation."

For me, all these beautiful verses in the Bible record convictions of how precious human beings are. They are "crowned with glory and honour", that is, to put it in modern language, every human has an intrinsic dignity which may not be violated. Every human being, male and female, manifests the image of God and is therefore to be respected as a whole. If this is what Christians are convinced of, then we are not only committed to an understanding of the preciousness of human persons, but also commit ourselves to defend this very dignity in every human person, particularly in those whose rights to it are crushed by violence or by systematic forces of oppression.

God's image and Asian realities

How do we read these biblical verses in the context of Asian societies? What does it mean to live in that full humanity which is expressed by the presence of the divine image in us? What are the major issues threatening the dignity and nobility of the humanity of our brothers and sisters in Asian societies? Here I want to go back to the very flesh and bone of Asian theology, the Asian contexts in which Asian Christians read their Bible.

Most Asian countries today are still suffering from neo-colonial economic structures, in which transnational corporations and international monetary systems exploit both their natural and human resources. Many Asian governments are in collaboration, militarily and otherwise, with these transnational business operations. Moreover, we are caught in the cultural contradiction between old traditional values, which have to be re-interpreted, and the flux of Western values, which also need constructive critical analysis.

Among the most oppressed victims are Asian women. The image of the subservient and servile Asian woman is further exploited in the various forms of trafficking, ranging from mail-order brides to prostitution. National economic crises impose a double burden on Asian women in the work situation (low wages and sexual harassment), and they bear a triple burden of managing their jobs, taking care of their homes and caring for their children. In cases of political repression, over and above the physical torture that their male comrades face, women political dissidents are raped and sexually tortured.

The dehumanization of people, especially the economically and politically powerless, is commonplace in Asia. Marginalized groups such as tribal people, people of low class or caste and women are the ones most oppressed both by the international economic system and by the systems at home. In the following, I shall highlight some of the dehumanizing situations in Asia in order to place our understanding of the Bible and of our faith in a fuller context.

After studying abroad for a few years, I recently visited friends at the Christian Labour Church in Hong Kong, where I previously served on the staff. This has been an active community, including people who suffered from unfair dismissal, women and children whose husbands and fathers had been disabled or killed in industrial accidents, and middle-aged workers who had lost their jobs because of the Hong Kong government's decision to import labour from China. My visit was rather depressing, for their economic situation, despite years and years of hard labour, is only worsening.

I remember in particular one woman worker who had been in the garment factories since the age of 12. Until recently, when her brother and sister got married, she had been supporting a family of six. While she still has to support her aged parents and a younger brother who is mentally disabled, she has been unemployed for almost a year, since most garment factories have moved to China, where operating costs are low and labour is cheap. When she was young she had been told that she would never have to worry about her livelihood if she could use a sewing machine and worked hard. Yet although she learned the most sophisticated sewing and became a team leader in her factory, she is now left with no job in her early forties. Now she has no competitive skill, no future and no security. She has become one more Hong Kong worker betrayed by society because she is no longer needed for the prosperity of that society.

While the workers on whom the prosperity of Hong Kong today was built have been abandoned, those in China, to where the Hong Kong manufacturers have shifted, are being greatly exploited. They receive low pay for long hours of work and suffer from very poor living and working conditions as the Hong Kong manufacturers take advantage of the great demand for jobs there. In Shenzhen, one of the fastest-growing economic zones of China, more than 80 workers died and many others were injured in a fire not long ago inside a factory dormitory. All the windows were locked; the dormitory had no fire exit; and the stairs were filled with goods. So when the fire broke out there was no way of escape for the workers inside.

Six years earlier I was involved in helping the victims of a fire in a leather factory in Hong Kong. Compared to the one in Shenzhen, it had few casualties. But I will never forget the horror of sitting outside the emergency ward of the hospital, waiting for the doctor to come out to announce another death, and seeing the families suffering greatly from watching their loved ones struggling in pain, fighting to breathe for another day. The people who had over 70-80 percent burns have literally been deformed.

The women workers who died or were injured in the Shenzhen fire had been sent there by their families from the poor provinces in China. The two million Chinese workers who have migrated from the interior to the Pearl River delta in southeast China are part of the large flow of migrant workers in Asia. It is estimated that more than 3.5 million migrant workers come out of the Philippines alone. Hong Kong itself has received around 35,000 Filipinos. Most of these migrant workers are women.

This large-scale trafficking of women as a work force happens in countries such as Taiwan, China, Thailand and the Philippines. Women from the poor countryside are sent away to the cities or overseas to work in all kinds of jobs: in factories, in people's homes as domestic workers and, often without knowing it beforehand, as dancers and prostitutes. Worst of all, behind all this trafficking in women migrant workers, the governments of the supplying countries collaborate with the agents of the tourist industry, usually perpetuating the business because of the large economic profit they can get from it. All the Asian countries which encourage women migrant workers list tourism and foreign remittances from migrant workers as major sources of national income. In other words, without ever being acknowledged by governments, many of these women are sacrificed in order to build up the national economy of their home countries.

Another example of people being degraded or dismissed as unimportant in the name of economic or national development is the Adivasi or tribal people in India. Thousands of Adivasi villagers have been displaced from the Narmada Valley in central India by the construction of a dam. There is a similar case in the upper valley of the Yangtze River in China. Peoples of different countries are facing the same fate of being displaced from the home of their ancestors and having to give up the land, the culture and the livelihood upon which their identities depend. In the name of development, the authorities drown millions of hectares of land by building large dams which benefit a few rich people, while ignoring the cries of the poor majority who are losing their security and dignity.

The suffering servant: rereading Isaiah

These few cases represent only a small sample of the general situation that many marginalized Asian communities face. And it is in comprehending the realities of the Asian peoples' sufferings that we seek to understand our Christian faith, especially what it means to be full human beings created in the image of God.

For me, this experience of deprived communities in Asia sheds new light on the suffering servant in Isaiah 53. Very different from the traditional Christian messianic interpretation of the servant, I see here a vivid portrayal of the sufferings of the marginalized communities in Asia. It speaks from among the middle-aged and old workers in Hong Kong, the women migrant workers in cities and overseas and the internally displaced tribal peoples in different Asian countries.

When we look at the description of the suffering servant from the angle of the sufferings of marginalized communities, we begin to see our relationship with them in a new light. More than other members of society, the marginalized are "marred... beyond human semblance" and their forms are "beyond that of mortals" (52:4). Like the suffering servant in Isaiah 53, the Adivasi, the Aboriginals and the poor villagers are "like a root out of dry ground", "despised and rejected by others" and made to become persons of "suffering..., acquainted with infirmity" (53:2f.). In 53:4-5, instead of being redeemed by us Christians as part of the privileged class in our society, the marginalized communities have actually "borne our infirmities and carried our diseases"; it is they who are "wounded for our transgressions". They are suffering because of our silence, our negligence and, worse, our collaboration with the power structures — while we are actively acquiring property and wealth for our churches, our Christian premises or compounds.

While the marginalized communities are taken away "by a perversion of justice" and "cut off out of the land of the living, stricken for the transgression" of us people (53:8), verse 6 says God lays on them "the iniquity of us all". In other words, we are all responsible for the sufferings that have been laid on the men and women of these deprived communities, the workers, the tribals and the women migrant workers.

In Isaiah 53, we see how a despised and wounded human being is raised and lifted up by God. These suffering men and women in the deprived communities have risen up as God promised. There are streams of people's movements all over Asia. Because of the flooding of the Narmada Valley, thousands of Adivasi have joined hands in a national movement. Women's movements are emerging from systematic degradation as one of the strongest movements among the people. Isaiah 53:5 says that upon them "was the punishment that made us whole, and by [their] bruises we are healed". It is through the continuous struggle of these marginalized communities that we may learn to become whole and be healed of our wounds.

As biblical scholars continue to debate such questions as the "original" identity of this suffering servant, whether the servant's suffering was voluntary or not and whether the suffering was as an individual or as a representative of a larger community, what compels us most as Asian Christians, living in societies where the majority of our people suffer on a day-to-day basis, is the parallel between the severe suffering of our peoples and this servant in Isaiah 53.

Reading the suffering servant as deprived communities, rather than as Christians in the churches, helps us to see two points in rethinking the role of the ecumenical movement in the struggle of these communities. On the one hand, it points to the need to place the sufferings of the marginalized communities at the centre of the life of the church, since it is in them and through them that we find God's promise and the manifestation of God's redeeming power. On the other hand, it points to the need for confession. We as churches must confess our transgression, our sin of being, consciously and unconsciously, part of the existing power system that marginalizes and deprives our brothers and sisters and makes them suffer.

The full humanity of women

Since women are the primary victims in all systematic oppression of the marginalized, I would like to highlight the consistent denial of the full humanity of women. Reading the Bible and taking serious account of the oppression done to women at the same time is not an easy job. To hear God's voice one must dig underneath the layers of patriarchal cultures and tradition in the Bible. Although the Bible contains strong references to caring for the weak within our community, the particular sufferings of women have somehow to be lifted up in both the Old and New Testament.

In fact, it is not difficult to find texts that affirm the sacrifice of women for the interests of their community. One such story is found in Judges 19-20, which tells of a concubine who was sent out to a gang of men for the night in order to spare her master from getting into trouble. She was raped and abused until dawn, and when she struggled to go back to her master's place, she was left dying until daylight.

When her master discovered the body, he took it back to his home and cut it up, limb by limb, into twelve parts in order to show the twelve tribes how he had been insulted. Because of this, the tribes were united as "one man" and fought the tribe from which the gang came.

Here again, I am not particularly interested in the scholarly discussion of the historical factors that come to play in the telling of this story. Nor do I care why and how the tribes were united and formed into one nation afterwards. I see the story as one of the stories of horror. In a different form, it mirrors the situation of Asian women migrant workers. Women are used to support the national economy. They are encouraged to migrate to work in a foreign land, where they are often sexually harassed, physically abused or psychologically subjected to a mode of slavery. But the community and the nation who benefit from their work never recognize their contribution. Rather they continue to "cut them into pieces" by ignoring the need to protect their fellow women from being abused by working in a foreign land.

Disappointingly, in the story as recorded in the book of Judges, no mention is made of God's saying anything about the woman's death. Like many other women in Judges, she died for the sake of the unity of the other tribes. Like many other women in the Old Testament, she does not even have a name. And as long as the contribution of women in society is not recognized or acknowledged, women's sacrifices will continue to be taken for granted.

What does this mean for us as Christians in Asia, where the human dignity of deprived people is continually threatened and often violated? The situation of Asia requires us to look for the face of Jesus, for the image of God, amidst the sufferings of our communities. In Matthew 25:31ff., Jesus' face is the face of the imprisoned, the hungry, the thirsty, the homeless and the migrant. Perceiving the image of God in human beings is for us a task and a mission to take care of the least of our brothers and sisters.

* * *

I conclude by saying something about my Christian faith as a woman in Asia. As a religious institution planted mainly by colonial powers from Europe and North America, Christianity must undergo critical reflection by us as Asian Christians. This critical understanding of our faith tradition has to be grounded first of all in the historical experience of Asia, including the past and the present, in the cultural and religious contexts of Asian peoples (about which I have not said much here because of space limitations) and, finally, in the principle of the liberation of marginalized peoples, especially women.

The consequence of this is the courage to call into question the relevance of assigning the final authority to the Bible and the appropriation of certain doctrines and symbols. Only in this way will we as Asian Christians be able to account for what we believe in the Bible to have an integral relationship with what we are called to do in our societies. Only by doing this can we witness to our communities that the biblical religion is a living faith in Asia.

III

*The Meaning
of Being a People*

7. A Jewish Theology of Jewish Relations to Other Peoples

ELLIOT N. DORFF

Judaism as an evolving, religious civilization

The Jewish people is a complicated and complex phenomenon. Unlike most other peoples, the Jews cannot be defined by their occupancy of a particular piece of land. The name "Jews" comes from Judah, the part of modern Israel where they lived in ancient times, but for at least 2500 years the vast majority of Jews have not lived there, and even today the majority of the world's Jews live elsewhere. The Hebrew language is surely a defining element in Jewish identity, for it is the language of the Bible, Mishnah and prayerbook; but until the establishment of the modern State of Israel, Hebrew has not been the language Jews spoke on a daily basis since First Temple times (c. 950-586 BCE). The languages Jews have spoken, the foods they have eaten and the clothes they have worn have been determined instead by the particular places in which they found themselves — and that has been all over the world. All of the usual factors in defining a people, then, are skewed when it comes to the Jewish people.

One might then conclude that Jews are not a people, but a religion. Judaism is certainly a central element in the identity of Jews, but particularly in modern times there are many Jews who proudly affirm their Jewish identity but do not believe in the tenets of Judaism or obey its laws. Christians undoubtedly find this most peculiar, for one may be born into a Christian home and reared as a Christian, but one is only a Christian if one now believes that Jesus is the Christ. Adherence to the beliefs and practices of Judaism are not, in a similar way, a *sine qua non* for being part of the Jewish people.

The Jewish people, then, can neither be reduced to adherents of the Jewish religion nor neatly characterized as a nation like all other nations. Whatever category we use for them, in fact, will be not quite

right, for history has made the Jews a unique phenomenon. Mordecai
M. Kaplan (1881-1983) suggested that Judaism be seen as a *civilization* since it includes all the elements of a civilization;[1] and that may
be the best way to think of Jews. Thus, while the majority of the
world's Jews have not lived in Israel since First Temple times, there
have always been Jews there, and it has remained the land which Jews
throughout the ages have seen as their homeland, to which they longed
and prayed to return. Similarly, although Hebrew was not the first
language of Jews for most of Jewish history, it was always their
second language, primarily because it is the language of the prayerbook and the Bible. And while Jewish songs, dances, art, food and
clothing have been heavily influenced by the lands in which they
lived, all of these have ultimately flowed in recognizable ways from
the sources of the Jewish tradition.

Kaplan, though, did not characterize Judaism only as a civilization; he defined it as an *evolving, religious* civilization. The Judaism
of present times is not the same civilization as the Judaism of past
centuries, for Judaism is a living, evolving civilization. That does not
mean that there are no connections between the present forms of
Judaism and the past; quite the contrary, part of what makes current
forms of Judaism recognizably Jewish are the ties which Jews feel
towards their past and the substantive ways in which their concepts
and actions reflect those of Jews throughout history. Nor does the
evolving character of Judaism mean that the new forms are necessarily
better or will be longer lasting than the old ones; it is just that
contemporary conditions demand new embodiments of the Jewish
tradition which meet the needs of our time.

One of the ways in which civilizations differ from each other is in
the factors which become central to their identity as against those
which are more peripheral. Religion is central to the Jewish civilization, as Kaplan noted by defining it as an evolving, *religious* civilization. Thus, for example, the reason why Israel is the Jewish land is not
because most Jews have lived there for most of their history, but
because God promised it to Abraham and his descendants. The reason
why Hebrew is the Jewish language is because it is the language of
Jewish religious texts. Jews may adopt many kinds of cuisine, but
they are Jewish only if they follow the dietary (*kosher*) laws of the
Jewish religion.

Even if many contemporary Jews identify themselves as such primarily through other elements of the Jewish civilization, it is to the Jewish religion that we must turn to understand the identity of the Jewish people. And the Jewish religion is rooted in the covenant of the Jewish people with God.

A people apart, formed by a covenant with God

The Hebrew Bible describes the historical roots of the Jewish people in substantial detail, from Abraham and Sarah, to Moses and the Exodus from Egypt, to the eventual conquest of the Promised Land. For the Bible, though, it is not these historical events which constitute the *raison d'être* of the Jewish people; rather, it is the theological phenomenon that the Jews are called by God to enter into a covenant with him, with mutual promises and responsibilities. The history is not irrelevant; it is the stage on which the covenant is first made and on which it is to be carried out for all time. This is very much a covenant *within history*.[2] But it is the relationship with God which makes the historical events matter.[3]

According to the terms of the covenant, the Jews are obligated to be loyal to God and to love him, expressing that love primarily through obedience of God's commandments. These commandments demand that Jews live out God's will in the thick of life, not only in a cloistered environment like a synagogue or monastery, and that they teach them to their children and "recite them when you stay at home and when you are away, when you lie down and when you get up" (Deuteronomy 6:7). They are, in other words, to pervade one's life.

In return for such love and loyalty, God is to reward the love and obedience of the Jews with continued existence through progeny as numerous as the stars in the heaven, ownership of the land of Israel, material well-being and, probably the most important of all, a continued, special relationship to God. By contrast, failure to abide by the covenant will, the Bible assures us, produce the reverse: physical debilitations, loss of the Promised Land and detachment from God. But out of respect for the covenant, even if the people sin grievously, God will not abandon them forever but will rather forgive them and return them to the Promised Land and to the blessings of progeny and well-being. That is part of God's promise. God will do this also because God by nature is not only just, but loving and merciful.[4]

God's patience, though, is also a function of his own interest in preserving the covenant, for the people Israel were to be God's great experiment with humankind — God's "Chosen People" to be "a light of the nations", a model for all other peoples of what God really wants in his human creatures (cf. Exodus 19:5-6; Deuteronomy 7:6; 32:9; Isaiah 42:1-4; 49:6; 51:4). Consequently, God has a vested interest in having Israel as a Chosen People: apparently convinced that he cannot demand model behaviour from everybody, God nevertheless wants a group of people who can exemplify what living a godly way of life is all about. Israel is, as it were, the "honours class" in the school of humanity.

God's choice of Israel for this task is not based on any rational grounds; indeed, the Bible specifies that it is not because of Israel's greatness that God chose Israel for this task; on the contrary, Israel was among the smallest of peoples (Deuteronomy 7:7). Nor is it because of Israel's goodness. Shortly after making the covenant, the people abandon God for the molten calf (Exodus 32-34; cf. Deuteronomy 9:5ff.). They sin again in not trusting God to take them into the Promised Land after ten of the twelve spies report the difficulty of the task ahead (Numbers 13-14). In both cases, God seriously considers destroying the people forthwith and starting over again with Moses leading some other people, but Moses, using a series of lawyerly arguments, prevails on God to retain his ties with Israel. Thus size and trustworthiness are not the reasons for God's choice of Israel; it is rather because God loved Abraham, Isaac and Jacob and made promises to them that he agrees to continue his relationship with their descendants, no matter what.

Conversely, the people Israel also do not engage in this relationship for thought-out, rational reasons. They agree to the covenant amidst thunder and lightning at Mount Sinai — hardly an opportunity for free, coolly reasoned, informed consent (Exodus 19-24, esp. 24:7; Deuteronomy 5, esp. v. 24). The rabbis later tell two stories about this process. According to one, God went to all the other peoples of the world and offered them his covenant and they each refused when they found out some of its demands. Finally, as a last resort, God went to the insignificant people Israel, and they agreed to it without ever hearing its terms.[5] That is consent, but certainly not informed. The other story picks up on the biblical description of the awesome setting of Mount Sinai and says that God actually held the mountain over their heads and said, "Either accept the covenant, or this will be your burial place!"[6] On this account, Israel's consent to be God's covenanted people was both uninformed and coerced.

Clearly, then, it was irrational love on both sides that brought God and Israel into this special relationship. But it was to be a wedding with no possibility of divorce. God complains bitterly throughout the Bible of Israel's unfaithfulness; and, especially after the pogroms of the Middle Ages and the Holocaust in our own century, Jews have complained just as bitterly about God's failure to live up to his promise of protection and continuity. Some Jews, faced with these realities, have even converted to Islam or Christianity or, more recently, rejected Judaism for secularism or adopted an Oriental religion like Buddhism. The majority of Jews, however, continue in this relationship with God, however troubled it may be, and we believe that God continues with us as well.

Classical Judaism, in fact, does not grant Jews the option of leaving the covenant. Once a person is born to a Jewish mother or is converted to Judaism at age 13 or older, he or she is Jewish for life. A Jew who converts to another religion loses all privileges of being a Jew, such as marriage, burial and community honours, but retains all responsibilities of Jewish identity. "A Jew, even if he has sinned, is still a Jew," the Talmud says.[7]

This is because Jewish identity has never been defined by religious affirmations, although Judaism certainly has them; rather, being Jewish has historically been a function of being part of the Jewish people. Given the theological underpinnings of the covenant which called the people Israel into being, this might seem surprising, but it has been this way for at least two thousand years, if not from the time of the patriarchs. Since the Enlightenment, people in the West have been accustomed to thinking of nations as voluntary associations of individuals which anyone can choose to leave at any time, but Jewish peoplehood antedates such notions and has never accepted them. Instead, for Judaism all Jews, whether born or converted, are part of the Jewish people whether they like it or not, no matter what parts of the religion they affirm or deny and no matter how much of Jewish law they obey. Jewish identity, in other words, is a corporate identity of peoplehood which is as inescapable as one's body or eye colour. Some Jews may try to hide their Jewish identity, but it is still theirs.[8]

While some Jews may see this inextricable bond to the Jewish people as a burdensome trap, most Jews experience it as a great gift. No Jew need ever feel alone. Hillel, a first-century Jewish sage, said, "When I am here, everyone [of the Jewish people] is here."[9] That is not just a statement of ego on his part; it is a reflection of the strong bond all Jews feel towards each other. This is perhaps most dramatically felt at weddings and funerals, which Jews are commanded to attend to help the parties involved rejoice or mourn, but it is much more pervasive than that. Jews are supposed to pray, if at all possible, in the company of a quorum of ten Jews (a *minyan*); and Jewish law spells out a number of obligations which each Jew has to the local Jewish community and to the Jewish community worldwide. At times of persecution, that has involved massive, expensive and sometimes dangerous efforts to ransom captives and to relocate refugees to safe havens. But such duties to the community are not limited to emergencies; they pervade daily life. In other words, from the point of view of Judaism, one's very identity as an individual is a function of one's membership of the Jewish people. Early in the morning liturgy for each day, in fact, a Jew blesses God for having made him or her a Jew.

One is a Jew, then, on genealogical grounds, whether through physical birth to a Jewish woman or through rebirth as a Jew through conversion. But the substance of Jewish identity is not merely national or ethnic; on the contrary, it is highly theological and moral. Jews must retain their Jewish identity because of the awesome seriousness of their covenant with God and its goal, namely, modelling what a human society can and should be. Even in contemporary times, when a significant percentage of Jews does not consider itself religious, the sense of a unique role to play in making this a better world persists as a critical factor in Jewish self-understanding.[10]

This aspiration for the moral has evoked mixed reactions among other peoples. While some have admired Jews for the moral commitment born out of their covenantal relationship with God, most have resented the Jews for this, for it implicitly puts them in a lower status and makes them feel guilty.

This makes it imperative to point out the "normality" of the people Israel. With all other peoples of the world Jews share the usual goals of simply living life as it comes, hoping for some achievements and joys and carrying on the traditions of their ancestors. Especially after the Holocaust, Richard Rubenstein has emphasized, we Jews must remind other people of this, for, he maintains, the mediaeval pogroms and the Holocaust were caused at least in part by the fact that Christians forgot that we are normal and turned our chosenness inside out, making us not people struggling to be more godly but the very embodiment of Satan.[11] Consequently, we must state openly that the people Israel is, after all, a normal group, with the usual human needs, desires and foibles. But despite the Holocaust and despite modern secularism, the covenant idea is so deeply engrained in the Jewish tradition that it permeates the consciousness of most Jews, even those who do not consider themselves religious. Whether consciously or subconsciously, whether in its original theological form or in a new secular form, the covenant makes Jews strive to extend what human beings can *morally* and *humanly* achieve, thus making the Jewish people, as the Bible says, "a kingdom of priests and a holy nation" (Exodus 19:5-6). In so doing, it becomes, for better and for worse, what the Moabite seer Balaam described as "a people that dwells apart, not reckoned among the nations" (Numbers 23:9; Deuteronomy 32:12; 33:28; Jeremiah 49:31; Micah 7:14).

Nationalism and universalism

The national character of the covenant is clear-cut in both biblical and rabbinic literature. The covenant is specifically between God and the Jewish people; its terms do not apply to others:

> Now therefore, if you obey my voice and keep my covenant, you shall be my treasured possession out of all the peoples. Indeed, the whole earth is mine, but you shall be for me a priestly kingdom and a holy nation (Exodus 19:5-6).
>
> I the Lord am your God; I have separated you from the peoples... You shall be holy to me, for I the Lord am holy, and I have separated you from the other peoples to be mine (Leviticus 20:24,26; cf. Exodus 34:10; Leviticus 25:39-46; Deuteronomy 7:1-11; 10:12-22; 33:4; Jeremiah 11:1-13).

The rabbis continued this theme. Probably the best indication of this is what is said about the sabbath, which is the symbol of the ongoing covenant between God and Israel and thus, according to the rabbis, the equivalent of all the other commandments. [12] The Bible says: "The Israelites shall keep the sabbath, observing the sabbath throughout their generations as a perpetual covenant. It is a sign forever between me and the people of Israel..." (Exodus 31:16-17). On this the rabbis comment: "It [the sabbath] is a sign between me and you" (Exodus 31:17): that is, not between me and the other nations of the world (*Mekhilta*, Ki Tissa).

This was not simply a matter of ideology: it had a pervasive effect on practice as well. Like any other legal system, Jewish law assumes that its rights and obligations apply fully only to the members of the national group. The rabbis make this explicit by asserting that non-Jews are subject to only the seven commandments given to the children of Noah — prohibitions against murder, idolatry, incest, eating a limb torn from a living animal, blasphemy and theft and the requirement to establish laws and courts. [13] Non-Jews were given certain protections and privileges in Jewish law, as aliens often are in legal systems, but they were not required to take on "the yoke of the commandments" (a rabbinic expression) because that was exclusively a feature of God's covenantal relationship to the Jews. [14]

That part of the Jewish covenantal notion is fairly easy for Christians to understand because Christianity also conceives itself as the prime way of relating to God — indeed, as the "new covenant". What is more difficult to communicate is that for the Jewish tradition this did not mean (as it did for much of Christianity) that it was the only way for people to fulfill God's will for humankind and be "saved" (which has a very different meaning in Judaism from that in Christianity). Jews are required to obey the law because they are part of God's covenant with Israel at Sinai; [15] non-Jews were never part of the Sinai covenant and therefore they are not obligated under it. But this does not mean that they are excluded from God's concern or prevented from enjoying God's favour; on the contrary, if they abide by the seven commandments given to Noah and seek to be righteous, they have done all that God wants of them. "The pious and virtuous of all nations participate in eternal bliss," the rabbis said [16] — a sharp contrast to the eternal damnation inherited by those who reject Jesus according to some versions of Christianity. Even at the prime moment of nationalistic triumph, the Exodus from Egypt, the rabbis picture God rebuking the angels who are singing songs of praise over the destruction of the Egyptians in the Red Sea: "My children lie drowned in the sea and you sing hymns of triumph?"[17] Thus covenant does not entail exclusivity or triumphalism in Judaism.

But it is not easy to balance a sense of appreciation and pride in being God's covenanted people who follow God's preferred way with the firm belief that all people as God's creatures are the object of his concern and eligible for his favour. Depending on historical circumstances, it is inevitable that sometimes one of these tenets has been emphasized to the exclusion of the other. During the persecutions under the Roman emperor Hadrian, expressions of extreme antipathy could be heard, such as the remark of Simeon bar Yohai that "the best of Gentiles should be killed". On the other hand, during the more friendly atmosphere of early Sassanid Babylon, Samuel claimed that God makes no distinction between Israel and the nations on the Day of Judgment.[18] In other times and places, the balance that Judaism affirms reasserted itself.

Both the tensions and the balance are probably best illustrated in the Jewish notion of Messianism. The ultimate aim, as Isaiah declared, is that all people worship God, so that there will be universal peace among people and in nature, even to the extent that the lion will lie down with the lamb (Isaiah 2:2-4; 11-12). But Israel has a special role to play as "a light of the nations" (Isaiah 49:1-6; 51:4); and, as several biblical prophets asserted, it is Israel's God that all people will ultimately worship and Israel's Torah that they will practise (Isaiah 2:2-4; 19:23-24; Zephaniah 2:11; 3:8-9; Zechariah 14:9). Moreover, according to the rabbis, in Messianic times Jews will be rewarded for their efforts to make God's will known by the reunion of the tribes of Israel in the land of Israel, the rebuilding of Jerusalem, the restoration of Jewish political autonomy and general prosperity — to the extent that non-Jews will seek to convert to Judaism to take advantage of the Jews' new status but will not be allowed to do so because their motive is not disinterested:

> "You brought a vine out of Egypt" (Psalm 80:8). As the vine is the lowliest of trees and yet rules over all the trees, so Israel is made to appear lowly in this world but will in the hereafter inherit the world from end to end. As the vine is at first trodden under the foot but is afterwards brought upon the table of kings, so Israel is made to appear contemptible in this world... but in the hereafter the Lord will set Israel on high, as it is said,

"Kings shall be your nursing fathers" (Isaiah 49:23) (*Leviticus Rabbah* 36:2).

In the hereafter the Gentile peoples will come to be made proselytes but will not be accepted (*B. Avodah Zarah* 3b).

Thus those who are part of God's covenant with Israel are to enjoy special privileges for the added covenantal responsibilities they have borne, but ultimately all people are to participate in the human fulfillment of Messianic times and the hereafter.

The tension between national pride and universalist convictions evident in the biblical and rabbinic doctrine of the covenant is also manifest in modern treatments of the subject. For example, Franz Rosenzweig and Martin Buber affirm the two elements of the balance: Rosenzweig emphasizes the special character of Israel, Buber the universal aspirations of the covenant. In that sense the former is a "nationalist" and the latter a "universalist". A third resolution of this tension is the theory of Mordecai Kaplan that Jews ought to think of themselves not as *chosen*, which carries with it too many negative connotations about how they view non-Jews, but as having a specific *vocation* to carry out their own history and traditions, just as every other civilization does. [19] This preserves the national character of the Jewish people while enabling Jews to recognize in theory and in fact the unique character and special contributions of many nations and civilizations.

Idolaters and monotheists

The universalist tendencies within the Jewish tradition are especially remarkable in light of the beliefs and practices of the other peoples whom the biblical authors and the talmudic rabbis had in mind. Whether Canaanites or Romans, they were by and large not monotheists but idolaters. The Hebrew Bible is relentless in its campaign against idolatry, enshrining the prohibition against it within the Decalogue itself announced on Mount Sinai (Exodus 20:3-6; Deuteronomy 5:7-10). Moreover, according to the Torah, the reason why God wants the Israelites to occupy the Land of Israel and displace the seven nations there is because of their idolatry and consequent immorality (Genesis 15:16; Deuteronomy 9:4-5). Similarly, the rabbis devoted an entire tractate of the Mishnah and Talmud, *Avodah Zarah*, to ensuring that Jews would not get close enough to idolatry or idolaters even to be tempted by it. Some passages make fun of idolatry, and the rabbis wrote liturgies thanking God for enabling Jews to be among those who spend their time in studying and practising the Jewish tradition rather than wasting away their lives following the emptiness and immorality of idolatry. [20]

Why the Jewish tradition objects so strongly to idolatry is open to interpretation. The descriptions of idolatry in biblical and rabbinic sources make it clear that part of the reason is the grossly immoral practices — including adultery, incest and child sacrifice — which characterized the cultic life of idolatrous peoples of the ancient world and often carried over to their general lives as well (see Leviticus 18; 2 Kings 21:3-7; 23:4-12; Jeremiah 7:30-31). But there was undoubtedly a theological reason as well: worshipping the sun, moon and stars amounts to making part of reality the whole of it, taking one of God's creatures as God himself; the error is even more egregious if one makes an idol of a human artifact. Thus idolatry involved both theological and moral errors which made it impossible even to recognize, let alone properly to worship, God.

Nevertheless, it is precisely the idolaters of ancient times about whom the rabbis also said that the righteous among them shall inherit a place in the world to come. This of course has direct implications for the relationships of Judaism to truly idolatrous faiths in our time, like Hinduism. Judaism would never embrace their polytheism as a vision of the truth or their idolatry as appropriate worship, but there are elements within Jewish literature and theology which would demand respect for those who practise such religions as creatures of God and even acknowledge that there are undoubtedly righteous people among them.

If this is true for polytheists, how much more for monotheists. Consequently, mediaeval Jewish sources, recognizing the strict monotheism of Islam, did not apply the laws against idolatry to Muslims. Because of the doctrine of the Trinity and the practice among some Christians of bowing before holy relics and statues of saints, mediaeval Jewish sources were less sanguine about Christianity; but some, especially Rabbi Menahem Meiri (1249-1316), understood Christianity as monotheistic as well. [21] Clearly, Christian persecution of Jews in many times and places did little to encourage such positive evaluations of Christianity, but even within that context some rabbis understood the monotheism at the heart of Christianity and modern rabbis have done so with increasing regularity.

Jews' relations to other religions: the groundwork

With these classical understandings of the nature and mission of the Jewish people, how should contemporary Jews relate to people of other faiths? The primary issue here is not such generally human concerns as matters of justice or commerce, for in these areas what governs for Jews are Jewish conceptions of God as the creator of us all and Jewish laws insisting that all peoples be treated fairly. Later Jewish law went further: to establish good relations with non-Jews, Jews must help the poor and the sick of all peoples and aid in burying their dead and in comforting the mourners. [22] Such humanitarianism is not characteristic of many interactions among peoples in the modern world. Moreover, the ways in which Christians and others persecuted Jews throughout history make this high standard of civility in traditional Judaism remarkable: Jewish theology, unlike some forms of Christian and Muslim theology, did not blind Jews to the human necessity of being honest, fair and caring towards those who believed differently.

The deeper question is a theological one: how do Jews understand the truth-status of other religions? Are other peoples simply deluded, or might their religions contain truths from which Jews can themselves learn? But if other religions do contain truth, why (apart from family and historical considerations) should Jews remain Jewish?

The same question of course arises *within* the Jewish community, for pluralism there, too, requires justification. [23] After all, if I think I know the truth about what is and what ought to be, why should I tolerate, let alone appreciate, the mistakes of others, whether they be members of my people or not? Answering that question clearly and convincingly is absolutely critical if we are ever to move beyond persecuting or merely tolerating others to the point of actually understanding and appreciating them.

It seems to me that there are historical, philosophical and theological grounds for such pluralism in relations between Jews and people of other faiths:

1. *History*. Historically, Christianity has been subject to at least as much change and redefinition as Judaism, if not more. Even within

the same denomination, creeds created centuries ago are continually changed, sometimes through outright amendment and sometimes through new interpretations, emphases or applications. This constantly evolving nature of both Judaism and Christianity makes some of the faithful uneasy; they long for certainty and stability. But each religion retains its relevance and dynamism only by opening itself to change.

In any case, like it or not, the historical fact is that both religions *have* changed and continue to change. Today's certainties, *even within the boundaries of one's own faith*, are not necessarily tomorrow's convictions. One need only think of the many ways in which one's beliefs or practices differ from those of one's ancestors to see this evolutionary point. The same holds true for one's understandings of others. The Second Vatican Council's repudiation of blaming Jews then or now for the death of Jesus and the recent rejection by the Lutheran denominations in North America of Luther's many anti-semitic writings are relevant cases in point.

At the same time, history does not undermine one's ability to take a strong stand on what one believes, and it certainly does not prevent a community from drawing boundaries. For example, even though the contemporary Jewish community is much exercised over the question of who is a Jew, it has uniformly and authoritatively determined that groups like Jews for Jesus are decidedly *not* Jews. The historically evolutionary nature of both faiths should, however, help contemporary Jews and Christians get beyond the feeling that the present articulation of their faith is the only one possible for a decent person to have; on the contrary, history should teach us that people of intelligence, morality and sensitivity most likely exist in other faiths too.

Awareness of Asian faiths should, if anything, make this point all the more compelling. Because Eastern faiths are not our own and have not had a long history of conflict with us, we can probably see all the more clearly the historical evolution of their ideas and practices and the influences from outside which have affected them through the ages. That may help us to recognize the same process of development in our own religions, for which we too have taken a little from here and a little from there in shaping what has come down to us as our particular form of Judaism or Christianity. That should convince us not to be so certain that the present articulation of our convictions must inevitably be — or even empirically will be — the only possible way for people of intelligence and moral sensitivity.

2. *Philosophy.* This realization is reinforced when one turns to philosophical considerations. All human beings, whatever their background or creed, operate within the same limitations on human knowledge. For many of us, our sacred texts and traditions reveal the nature and will of God (or, in the case of non-theological traditions, ultimate reality) as clearly and fully as we think possible. But when we recognize that other peoples make the same claim, we must either resort to vacuous and inconclusive debates about whose tradition is right or confront the inability of any of us to know God's nature or will with absolute certainty.

At the same time, philosophical factors do not — any more than historical considerations — make a specific faith impossible or inadvisable. We may think our particular understanding of God is the correct one for all people, *as far as we can tell*, and we may advance arguments to convince others of this, even though we know ahead of time that no human argument on these matters can be conclusive.

Alternatively, we may take a more "live and let live" approach, recognizing that part of the persuasiveness for me of the arguments for my faith is that it is *my* faith and that of my family and my people. Such a position does not necessarily deny cognitive meaning to religion, as A.J. Ayer, R.B. Braithwaite and others did in the middle of this century;[24] it need only be a humble recognition that none of us is an objective observer, that we all view the world from a vantage point and that our autobiographical background inevitably plays — and perhaps should play — a role in which viewpoint is ours.

One could be, in Van Harvey's terminology, a "soft perspectivist" rather than a "hard perspectivist" or "non-perspectivist". In other words, one can say, against "non-perspectivism", that all of us do have a point of view which influences how we think and act; we do not look at the world through epistemologically transparent spectacles. At the same time, one may add, against "hard perspectivism", that our point of view need not blind us to other perspectives; indeed, we can possibly learn from the views of others.[25]

The latter approach would make for a much stronger foundation for mutually respectful Jewish-Christian relations, but even the former view, with its open recognition of the limits on what anyone can know of God, holds promise. That is because both views come out of a philosophically accurate assessment of our knowledge of God: we can and do say some things about God and act on our convictions, and our beliefs and actions can be justified by reasons which can be shared and appreciated by others; but other, equally rational, moral and sensitive people might differ with us and might also have good reasons for what they say and do. This is only to be expected in an area in which our knowledge is, by the very nature of the knower and the subject to be known, incomplete.

Asian faiths underscore this point, for by and large they have not been nearly as exclusive as the Western faiths have historically been. They have rather stated their convictions and practices and left it to individuals to adhere to them or to other faiths as they choose. Westerners accustomed to an "either-or" approach to truth in both philosophy and religion feel decidedly uncomfortable with such a "both-and" approach. The epistemological humility for which I am arguing, however, and which I see as the only philosophically responsible position to take, should goad us to learn an important lesson from our Asian brothers and sisters.

3. *Theology.* In addition to these historical and philosophical considerations, some important Jewish theological tenets can be used to lay the groundwork for a genuinely pluralistic appreciation of others.

The Mishnah, the central collection of rabbinic law from the first and second centuries, asks why God initiated the human species by creating only one man (Adam). One reason, the Mishnah suggests, is to impress upon us the greatness of the Holy One, blessed be he, for when human beings mint coins, they all come out the same, but God made one mold (Adam) and yet no human being looks exactly like another. This physical pluralism is matched by an intellectual pluralism for which, the rabbis say, God is to be blessed: "When one sees a crowd of people, one is to say, 'Blessed is the Master of mysteries', for just as their faces are not alike, so are their thoughts not alike."

The Midrash, the written record of rabbinic lore, supports this further. It says that when Moses was about to die, he said to the Lord: "Master of the universe, you know the opinions of everyone and that there are no two among your children who think alike. I beg of you that after I die, when you appoint a leader for them, appoint one who will bear with [accept, *sovel*] each one of them as he thinks [on his own terms, *lefi da'ato*]." We know that Moses said this, the rabbis claim, because Moses describes God as "God of the *ruhot* [spirits, in the plural] of all flesh" (Numbers 24:16). [26] Thus God *wants* pluralism so that people will constantly be reminded of his grandeur.

Moreover, according to the rabbis, God intentionally reveals only a part of his truth in the Torah and the rest must come from study and debate. [27] Even with study there is a limit to human knowledge, for as the mediaeval Jewish philosopher Joseph Albo said, "If I knew him, I would be he." [28]

God as understood in the Jewish tradition thus wants pluralism not only to demonstrate his grandeur in creating humanity with diversity, but also to force human beings to realize their epistemological creatureliness, the limits of human knowledge in comparison to that of God. From the standpoint of piety, pluralism emerges not from relativism, but from a deeply held and aptly humble monotheism.

There are some limitations to this line of reasoning as the basis for Jewish relations to other faiths. It may be the case that God wants us to think independently, but ultimately the biblical prophets assert that the Torah is God's true teaching, the one which all nations will ultimately learn. Micah, for example, a younger contemporary of Isaiah, copies the latter's messianic vision but then adds a line of his own which effectively changes it: "Though all the peoples walk each in the names of its gods, we will walk in the name of the Lord our God forever and ever" (Micah 4:5; compare Micah 4:1-3 with Isaiah 2:2-4). This is a decidedly pluralistic vision of Messianic times: every people shall continue to follow its own god. Even so, Micah added this line *after* quoting Isaiah's vision that "many peoples shall come and say: 'Come, let us go up to the mountain of the Lord, to the house of the God of Jacob, that he may teach us his ways and that we may walk in his paths'. For out of Zion shall go forth instruction, and the word of the Lord from Jerusalem" (Isaiah 2:3; Micah 4:2). Thus even for Micah, apparently, other gods and other visions of the good life might exist, but it is only Israel which has the true understanding of God's will.

In sum, God may indeed want multiple conceptions of the divine, but traditional sources assign non-Jewish views to a clearly secondary status. God may like variety among his creatures and he may even hold people responsible only for what they could be expected to know (the seven Noahide laws); but ultimately only the Jews know what is objectively correct. This is liberal toleration — and it should be appreciated as such — but it certainly is not a validation of others' views. In that sense, it falls short of what Simon Greenberg, a contemporary Conservative rabbi, suggests as a criterion for genuine pluralism: that "your ideas are spiritually and ethically as valid — that is, as capable of being justified, supported and defended — as mine."[29] Indeed, Greenberg himself may not have wanted to extend his thesis beyond disagreements among Jews.

I would take a somewhat broader view. It is only natural that Jewish sources cited earlier should reflect a tension between nationalism and universalism. God is, according to Jewish belief, the God of all creatures, but, at the same time, he chose the Jews to exemplify the standards he really wants for human life. This is how *Jews* understand God's will, the reason why they commit all their energies and indeed their very lives to Jewish belief and practice.

Despite this nationalistic side of the Jewish tradition, however, what ultimately rings through it are the rabbis' assertions that non-Jews fully meet God's expectations by abiding by the seven Noahide laws and that "the pious and virtuous of all nations participate in eternal bliss". Thus Jewish sources which speak about God wanting plural approaches to him within the Jewish community can apparently also be applied, without too much tampering, to inter-communal relations. Of course, the same segments of the Jewish community which have difficulty with the former would undoubtedly have difficulty with the latter, and even some pluralists within the Jewish community would need to stretch their understanding and sensitivity to apply Jewish theology in this way. Nevertheless, a firm basis for this kind of theology exists within the Jewish tradition.

A realistic but open model of the covenant for our times

If Jews are to stretch in this way, they justifiably can expect Christians and others to do likewise. I personally have no doubt that Christians and others *can* find the requisite sources within their own tradition to do this if *they choose to do so*. Indeed, we must all develop the strands in each of our traditions which recognize that people with opinions differing from our own may be moral and intelligent and even have something to teach us about the true and the good. Recognition of the historical development of each of our traditions should help us to see that our contemporary understanding of things may not be ultimately correct, and attention to the philosophical limits of our knowledge should disabuse us even further of our claims to certainty. Within Judaism as well as many other faiths, theological concerns would also support such a move towards openness to others and the lessons they have to teach us.

In other words, universalism in our own day involves the recognition that God can and does relate to all people. The particular way in which God does this may vary, and it is inevitable that people will feel that their own approach is best, but this should not produce the conclusion that other paths to God are necessarily bad, ineffective or unauthentic. It may well be that God wisely entered into different forms of relationship with different peoples to fit the traditions, talents and sensitivities of each group. It may also be that God has planned different roles for each group. Franz Rosenzweig suggested that the divine task of Jews is to model what God wants and the divinely ordained task of Christians is to carry the message to the Gentiles; the respective numbers of the Jewish and Christian communities and their respective policies on missionizing seems to support such a view. As Seymour Siegel has said:

> If this suggestion were to be accepted by Jew and Christian, it would be possible to open a new era of dialogue and mutual enlightenment. Christians would not denigrate Judaism by viewing it as a vestige, an anachronism of ancient times. They would cease their missionizing activities vis-a-vis Jews. For Jews there would be a new recognition of the importance of Christianity, of its spiritual dimension and its task to bring the word of God to the far islands. [30]

In any case, the ultimate goal in speaking to one another is not to synthesize all the traditions of the world into one or to ignore the real differences among them. It is to make those differences the source of genuine understanding of and learning from one another, rather than of the wars and persecutions that have all too often plagued us.

In this process, Jews will remain a people apart, committed to their mission of being a light to the nations, modelling our own understanding of God's will. In doing this, we will be carrying out the duties of our own covenant with God. As the Psalmist says:

O offspring of his servant Abraham,
children of Jacob, his chosen ones.
He is the Lord our God;
his judgments are in all the earth.
He is mindful of his covenant forever,
of the word that he commanded, for a thousand generations,
the covenant that he made with Abraham,
his sworn promise to Isaac,
which he confirmed to Jacob as a statute,
to Israel as an everlasting covenant (Psalms 105:6-10).

NOTES

The following common notations are used in citations of the classical rabbinic texts: M.
= Mishnah (ed. c. 220 C.E.); T. = Tosefta (ed. about the same time); J. = Jerusalem (or
Palestinian) Talmud (ed. approximately 400 C.E.); B. = Babylonian Talmud (ed. c. 500
C.E.); M.T. = *Mishneh Torah*, a code of Jewish law by Maimonides (1177 C.E.); S.A. =
Shulhan Arukh, a code of Jewish law by Joseph Karo (1565 C.E.) with notes by Moses
Isserles.

[1] Mordecai M. Kaplan, *Judaism as a Civilization*, New York, Reconstructionist Press,
1934; cf. *The Religion of Ethical Nationhood*, New York, Macmillan, 1970.
[2] For a mediaeval view of the importance of historicity see Judah Halevi, *Kuzari*, I, 11-43,
tr. in *Three Jewish Philosophers*, Philadelphia, Jewish Publication Society, 1960, III,
pp.33-37; for a contemporary interpretation, Emil Fackenheim, *God's Presence in
History: Jewish Affirmations and Philosophical Reflections*, New York, New York U.P.,
1970; and *The Jewish Return into History: Reflections in the Age of Auschwitz and a New
Jerusalem*, New York, Schocken, 1978.
[3] On the theological and legal implications of the covenant idea for contemporary Jewish
self-understanding, see my articles "Judaism as a Religious Legal System", *Hasting's
Law Journal*, vol. 29, July 1978, pp.1331-60; "The Meaning of Covenant: A Contemporary Understanding", in Helga Croner and Leon Klenicki, eds, *Issues in the Jewish-
Christian Dialogue*, New York, Paulist Press, 1979, pp.38-61; "The Covenant: The
Transcendent Thrust in Jewish Law", *The Jewish Law Annual*, vol. 7, 1988, pp.68-96;
on efforts by two modern Jewish theologians to reshape the covenant idea to account for
past and present relations with non-Jews, see "The Covenant: How Jews Understand
Themselves and Others", *Anglican Theological Review*, vol. 64, no. 4, October 1982,
pp.481-501.
[4] These themes occur often in the Bible. For the promises see Gen. 15; 17; 26:1-5,23-24;
28:13-15; 35:9-12; repeated, along with the curses for not fulfilling the terms of the
covenant, in, e.g., Lev. 26; Deut. 6-7; 11:13-25; 28. That God will punish disobedience
not only with physical deprivation and affliction but also with his absence is most clear in
the prophetic writings, e.g., Isa. 29:10; Jer. 7:1-15; Ezek. 7:23-27; Amos 8:11-12; Hosea
3:4; 5:6; Micah 3:6-7; Lam. 2:9.

[5] *Sifre Deuteronomy*, par. 343; *Numbers Rabbah* 14:10.

[6] B. *Shabbat* 88a; B. *Avodah Zarah* 2b.

[7] B. *Sanhedrin* 44a.

[8] Milton R. Konvitz has explicated this well; see *Judaism and the American Idea*, New York, Schocken, 1978, pp.139-59. See also my article, "Training Rabbis in the Land of the Free", in Nina Beth Cardin and David Wolf Silverman, eds, *The Seminary at 100*, New York, The Rabbinical Assembly and the Jewish Theological Seminary of America, 1987, pp.11-28.

[9] B. *Sukkah* 53a.

[10] In the USA, a 1988 *Los Angeles Times* national survey showed that more than half of Jews considered commitment to social equality as the quality most important to their sense of Jewish identity, whereas only 17 percent cited religious observance. Jewish lawyers make up a hugely disproportionate number of those who do *pro bono* work for the indigent: cf. Donna Arzt, "The People's Lawyers", *Judaism*, vol. 35, no. 1, 1986, pp.47-62; Jerold S. Auerbach and Donna Arzt, "Profits or Prophets: An Exchange", *ibid.*, vol. 36, no. 3, 1987, pp.360-367; and the percentage of Jews who contribute to charity and the percentage of income contributed far exceeds the US norm; cf. Edward S. Shapiro, "Jews With Money", *ibid.* vol. 36, no. 1, 1987, pp.1-16; Gerald Krefatz, *Jews and Money: The Myths and the Reality*, New Haven, Conn., Ticknor and Fields, 1982, ch. 11.

[11] Richard Rubenstein, *After Auschwitz*, Indianapolis, Bobbs-Merrill, 1966, chs.1-3, esp. pp.58, 69-71. For a radical rethinking of the nature of the covenant after the Holocaust by an Orthodox rabbi, see Irving Greenberg, *The Jewish Way*, New York, Simon & Schuster, 1988, ch.3, esp. pp.87-93.

[12] Cf. J. *Nedarim* 38b; *Exodus Rabbah* 25:12.

[13] T. *Avodah Zarah* 8:4; B. *Sanhedrin* 56a, 60a.

[14] These privileges and protections included giving charity to the non-Jewish poor and personal obligations like burying their dead, attending their funerals, eulogizing their deceased and consoling their bereaved; cf. M. *Gittin* 5:8; T. *Gittin* 5:4-5; and my article, "Jewish Perspectives on the Poor", in *The Poor Among Us: Jewish Tradition and Social Policy*, New York, American Jewish Committee, 1986, pp.21-55.

[15] See, e.g., Deuteronomy 7:9-11; *The Haggadah of Passover*, ed. Philip Birnbaum, New York, Hebrew Publishing Company, 1953, p.95.

[16] *Sifra* on Leviticus 19:18.

[17] B. *Megillah* 10b.

[18] Simeon bar Yohai in J. *Kiddushin* 4:11 (66c); Samuel in J. *Rosh Hashanah* 1:3 (57a). Cf. Daniel Sperber and Theodore Friedman, "Gentile", *Encyclopedia Judaica*, vol. 7, pp.410-14, which points out that the Jew's attitude towards the Gentile was largely conditioned by the Gentile's attitude toward him (see, e.g., *Esther Rabbah* 2:3). Moreover, to the extent that there was Jewish antipathy towards Gentiles, it was never based upon racial prejudice, but rather motivated by Gentiles' idolatry, moral laxity, cruelty to Jews and rejection of the Torah.

[19] On Rosenzweig and Buber, see my article, "The Covenant: How Jews Understand Themselves and Others", *loc. cit.*, esp. pp.484-93; on Kaplan, see my article, "The Meaning of Covenant: A Contemporary Understanding", *loc. cit.*, pp.40-46.

[20] Cf. B. *Avodah Zarah* 2ff.; J. *Berakhot* 7d.

[21] The Tosafists say outright that "we are certain that the Christians do not worship idols" (Tos. to B. *Avodah Zarah* 2a, s.v. *asur*), but due to their trinitarianism they do not see them as full monotheists and classify them instead as Noahides who are not enjoined against trinitarian belief (Tos. to B. *Sanhedrin* 63b, s.v. *asur*; Tos. to B. *Bekhorot* 2b, s.v. *Shema*). R. Menahem Meiri sees Christians as monotheists: *Beit Ha-Behirah* to B. *Bava Kamma* 113b and to B. *Avodah Zarah* 20a. Maimonides, on the other end of the spectrum, applies all the strictures against idolatry to Christians: M.T. *Laws of Idolatry* 9:4 (deleted by censors in the ordinary editions). A good summary of this can be found in the article, "Gentile", *Encyclopedia Judaica*, vol. 7, pp.410-14.

[22] According to the Talmud, the commandment to love the stranger and not to wrong him occurs 36 times in the Torah (see Hertz, *op. cit.*, p.314; e.g., Exodus 22:20; 23:9; Deuteronomy 9:19; and, perhaps most explicitly, Leviticus 19:33-34). Furthermore, "There shall be one law for the citizen and for the stranger who dwells among you" appears often in the Torah (e.g., Exodus 12:49; Leviticus 24:22; Numbers 15:15-16). These principles, together with the need to avoid the enmity of non-Jews, made Jews treat non-Jews with the same principles of justice that they used for themselves and even to bury the non-Jewish dead and to provide for the basic needs of the non-Jewish poor. On obligations to non-Jews see B. *Gittin* 61a; M.T. *Laws of Gifts to the Poor* 7:7; *Laws of Idolatry* 10:5; *Laws of Mourning* 14:12; *Laws of Kings* 10:12; S.A. *Yoreh De'ah* 335:9, 367:1.

[23] Elliot N. Dorff, "Pluralism", in Steven T. Katz, ed., *Frontiers of Jewish Thought*, Washington, B'nai Brith Books, 1992, pp.213-33.

[24] A.J. Ayer, *Language, Truth, and Logic*, London, Dover, 1936, pp.114-120; R.B. Braithwaite, "An Empiricist's View of the Nature of Religious Belief", reprinted in Ian T. Ramsey, ed., *Christian Ethics and Contemporary Philosophy*, New York, Macmillan, 1966, pp.53-73.

[25] Cf. Van A. Harvey, *The Historian and the Believer*, New York, Macmillan, 1966, pp.205-30; see also James W. McClendon Jr and James M. Smith, *Understanding Religious Convictions*, Notre Dame, Indiana, Univ. of Notre Dame Press, 1975, pp.6-8.

[26] The Mishnah cited is M. *Sanhedrin* 4:5; the blessing cited is in B. *Berakhot* 58a; and the Midrash cited is in *Midrash Tanhuma* on Numbers 24:16.

[27] J. *Sanhedrin* 22a; *Midrash Tanhuma*, ed. Buber, Devarim, 1a; *Numbers Rabbah* 19:6.

[28] Joseph Albo, *Sefer Ha-Ikkarim*, part II, ch.30, tr. Isaac Husik, Philadelphia, Jewish Publication Society of America, 1946, vol. II, p.206.

[29] Simon Greenberg, "Pluralism and Jewish Education", *Religious Education*, vol. 81, 1986, p.23; cf. p.27, where Greenberg links pluralism to the absence of violence in transforming another person's opinion.

[30] Seymour Siegel, "Covenants — Old and New", *Jewish Heritage*, spring 1967, pp.54-59. Rosenzweig's suggestion appears in *The Star of Redemption*, tr. William W. Hallo, New York, Holt Rinehart & Winston, 1971, Part III, Books I and II; cf. esp. p.166.

8. People of God and Peoples of God: Asian Christian Discussions

ISRAEL SELVANAYAGAM

"People of God" has been a central theme in theological discussions among Asian Christians. Obviously, this theme is taken from the Bible, which is not only the scripture of the Christians but also contains the scripture of the Jewish people. Since the Jewish people continue to define themselves as the people of God, some Jews find it difficult to accept the way in which Christians of the New Testament, both Jews and Gentiles, define themselves as "the new people of God" or as the extension of the people of God of the Old Testament. On this view, broadening the concept further to include other new categories of people as people of God will raise even more difficult and challenging questions.

The bibliography on discussions of the people of God in the Asian context is extensive. Papers and documents, monographs and essays, research and studies have been produced by the Christian Conference of Asia (CCA), the Ecumenical Association of Third World Theologians (EATWOT), the *Asian Journal of Theology*, the Programme for Theology and Cultures of Asia (PTCA), the Association for Theological Education in South East Asia (ATESEA) and the South Asia Theological Research Institute (SATHRI).

From among all the published materials on this subject, two items provide especially helpful summaries of and insightful commentaries on the full range of the discussion of "people of God" within the Asian context; and in what follows we shall limit our citations to these: Steven Mackie's essay "God's People in Asia: A Key Concept in Asian Theology",[1] hereafter cited as "Key Concept", and the report of an Asia mission conference in Osaka, Japan, in 1989,[2] hereafter cited as "AMC Report". Most of the other materials on the theme under review either repeat the concerns developed and discussed in these two sources or expand on them by identifying additional categories or sub-groups of people as "people of God" and describing their struggle and suffering.

The term "peoples" is significant as it denotes the plurality of Asian people, distinguished by geographical, cultural and ethnic identities. The Korean theologian Kim Yong-Bock draws out the implications of this plurality:

> The Asian horizon, culturally and religiously a rainbow with many visible and invisible colours, has not been clearly recognized in the Western colonial horizon dominated by the Western Christian worldview. But the national, religious and cultural identities and heritages of the Asian people and the diversity of their socio-economic and political contexts have been taken very seriously in Asia. So ecumenicity in Asia has not meant merely the unity of the churches and missions but the catholicity of the Christian community in embracing the people of different cultures and religions in their diverse socio-economic and political contexts ("AMC Report", p.6).

Such recognition of the plurality of the Asian context, says Kim Yong-Bock, entails "rejection and overcoming of the dichotomy of Western Christianity and pagan Asia" and the need for dialogue among different communities. According to Sri Lankan theologian Preman Niles, God's concern is not just the church (the *laos*) but all people (the *ochlos*) as well as the *ethne* ("AMC Report", p.58). Thus the category of people of God is extended across religious and ethnic frontiers. However, one particular kind of boundary is marked: the suffering people of Asia.

Suffering people as God's people

Suffering people are set apart for special recognition as people of God. They have distinctive names, stories, experiences and aspirations. Kim Yong-Bock notes:

> In Asia when we refer to the people, the *minjung*, the *janata*, etc. we are talking about the socio-economically poor, the politically oppressed, the religio-culturally alienated and suppressed. They are dalits, low caste and outcast people in India, oppressed ethnic minorities, colonized people. They do not have wealth, power, status in their own society. They suffer because of the structures that place them in unjust relationship with high-ranking or high-caste people... The system of injustice operates in

complex ways, and in shifting combinations. Under them the people suffer double and triple oppression, which ultimately drains their spiritual vitality ("AMC Report", pp.9f.).

The evil powers of political systems come upon the poor despite their resistance. In their struggle "to transform the oppressive dominating powers into servants of the people, not lords over them" (p.11), they need to participate in political decisions and economic planning. In sum, Kim Yong-Bock asserts, "the suffering and struggling peoples of Asia are the people of God. This is what we believe and confess" (p.13).

God's liberation of the Hebrew slaves in Egypt is then taken as a paradigm or root metaphor which can be applied to the suffering people of Asia. To quote Kim Yong-Bock again, "the God of the Exodus hears the cries of the suffering people in Asia. The God of the Hapiru (Egyptian slaves) promises liberation to the suffering people in Asia. The God of the prophets is the God of Asian history, which is full of injustice and suffering" ("AMC Report", p.12). Along the lines of the stories of the biblical people of God, the story of the Asian poor also unfolds as a story of the people of God. God moves and has being in their history, which reveals that they move and have their being in their suffering, struggles, hopes and aspirations.

Aloysius Pieris describes the people of the Third World as "the starving sons of Jacob — of all places and all times — who go in search of bread to a rich country, only to become its slaves". For him "the major focus of theology must be the Third World's irruption as a new peoplehood announcing the liberating presence of a God who claims to humanize the cruel world" ("Key Concept", p.222).

Moreover, the experience of suffering Asians is linked intrinsically to the story of Jesus Christ. According to Kim Yong-Bock, "Christian communities believe that the fundamental stream of the story of the peoples in Asia is being shaped by the story of Jesus Christ: Jesus is the Saviour and Messiah of the people in Asia. This paradigm determines the nature of the paradigm of the Christian witness among the people" ("AMC Report", p.8). Thus, Kim Yong-Bock says, we need to proclaim that Jesus is the Christ of the people of Asia since they belong to Christ:

> In suffering together with the Asian people, Christ finds his identity, and even his being in Asian history. This is the first dimension of solidarity of

Christ with the Asian people. It is messianic solidarity which is in
contrast to Christ as a political Messiah dominant over the people (p.16).

He goes on to point out how the Christian churches in Asia have
constricted Jesus Christ and thus excluded and alienated the people of
God, mainly through the power structures in the church. Jesus ate and
drank with the ordinary masses (*ochlos*) and identified with them on
the cross:

> The final and decisive Christology is manifested in the form of the
> hungry, the thirsty and the imprisoned (Matt. 25:31-46). This is the
> supreme Christology, in which the Christ and suffering people are
> indistinguishable. Christ is everywhere. Christ does not appear with
> special Christological titles, special ecclesial status or metaphysical
> justification. The presence of Christ is discerned where he is in solidarity
> with the suffering people. This is the supreme Christological mystery,
> abundantly transparent, but utterly unbelievable to the oppressor and the
> rich (p.16).

As suffering servant and victim, Christ is in solidarity with the victims
of political oppression and economic exploitation in Asia.

Also operative in the life and liberation of the suffering people of
God in Asia is the Spirit of God. They are given vitality, passion,
hope and vision by the Spirit of Pentecost and Jubilee, whose power
transforms the historical realities of death, injustice and darkness into
life, justice and shalom. The Spirit enables communication beyond
narrow particularities and brings solidarity for the people of God
("AMC Report", p.22). Thus in relating the God of the Exodus to the
suffering people in Asia, reference is profusely made to Jesus Christ
and the Holy Spirit, thereby completing the Christian pattern of
speaking of God.

People of God in the making

While the people of Asia are defined as people of God because of
their state as the suffering poor, Asian theologians also see them as
people in the making, again drawing on the biblical paradigm for
authenticity. Pieris says that "the Bible, as we understand it in our
Asian context, is the record of a *religious experience* of a 'non-people'
constantly struggling to be a 'people', a struggle in which God is an
intimate partner ("Key Concept", p.238).

Without focussing on the dialectical tension between God's owning and disowning of a people as recorded in the Bible, these Asian
Christian thinkers equate liberation with people in the making. In
other words, describing the suffering people of Asia as people of God
is the initial impetus for working out their liberation and fullness of
life. Again Kim Yong-Bock draws extensively on biblical descriptions:

> The mission of God among the suffering people of Asia is to restore life
> and dignity to the fullest, so that the image of God may be realized among
> them. God makes the poor socio-economically secure. God frees and
> liberates those oppressed and imprisoned by the dictatorial powers. God
> establishes justice, overthrowing the structures and systems of injustice.
> God gives peace to the refugees, the exiled people, the captives in the
> desolate, war-torn wastelands.
>
> God's household is established to secure the life of the suffering
> people, among whom God dwells. In God's dwelling among the people
> there is Shalom, not war, justice, not *han* (a deep sense of being
> wronged), there is freedom, not enslavement. God's work among the
> suffering people of Asia is the establishment of the *oikonomia* (house-
> hold, political economy) of God, in which the peoples of Asia may be
> socio-economically secure for fullness of their life..., culturally abundant
> life as well as a free and secure life in the society ("AMC Report",
> pp.12f.).

The precise nature of solidarity and community is also seen in the
light of biblical prescriptions and terms like "covenant" (faithful
relations), "koinonia" (sharing and communication) and "oikonomia"
(common living). "Solidarity is a form of sociality and community of
people for common living in justice and peace. The precise biblical
word for solidarity is *stereoma*, meaning steadfastness of community"
(p.30). The term "solidarity" is preferable to "unity", which remains
abstract. Solidarity requires full recognition of the subjecthood of
people and full confidence in relationship. "God commanded the
people of God to recognize God as Subject, and this implies that the
people of God are partners having subjecthood and selfhood" (p.31).

What is the role of the church in forming community and providing solidarity? The church as the body of Christ is supposed to
function as a community of peace: "the historical-sociological forma-
tion of the body of Christ or ecclesia or community of Christians is the

foundation... for the social body, that is, the community of the struggling and suffering people in Asia" (p.19). Christians are set free in order to serve the whole people of God in their diverse ethnicities. True communication develops when the Christians listen to peoples' stories.

With this brief summary of how the theme "people of God" is being used in Asian Christian theology, we turn now to three areas in which important issues and questions are raised by these reflections.

Continuity and discontinuity

While the Asian Christian thinkers we have consulted have not addressed the possible difficulties for Jewish-Christian dialogue in this application of the term "people of God" to all the suffering peoples of Asia, they are obviously aware that the paradigm comes originally from the Jewish religious tradition. Speaking of the "continuity and discontinuity between the Bible and the present situation", Preman Niles says the central problem for Asian Christians is "our understanding of the status of Israel, whether it be Israel of the Old Testament or the church as the New Israel. In the Bible the message of hope and salvation is addressed to Israel. The question arises as to what is the entity in Asia which is coterminous with the Israel of the Bible." Three possible answers, he says, are the Christian church as the New Israel, the poor and the suffering, and the whole of humankind ("Key Concept", pp.222f.). According to the "Transpositional Theology" of the Taiwanese theologian C.S. Song, "God has always been and will always be God for Israel and its peoples but at the same time has always been and will always be God for all nations and all peoples." Song defends this position by pointing to the New Testament rejection of the "centrism" of nation and of clan, and to the cross, which he says symbolizes the suffering and hope of all humanity. In the suffering of Asian peoples, Song finds God's own suffering:

> And God moves on... from the Tower of Babel to Pentecost, from Israel to Babylon. God moves in Europe, in Africa, in the Americas, in Asia. As God moves, God suffers with the people, sheds tears with them, hopes with them and creates the communion of love here and there... Until the time when the communion of love is firmly established in the world of strife and conflict, of pain and suffering, God moves on in compassion. We have no alternative but to move on with God towards that vision of a

community of compassion and communion of love ("Key Concept", p.230).

Pieris goes a step further in declaring that "the religiousness of the Asian poor (*who are largely non-Christian*) could be a source of revelation for the Asian church" (p.238).

Jewish people both past and present may have no difficulty affirming the movement of God in the history of Asian peoples. They may even be pleased to see their own story of suffering and liberation used to shed light on the story of Asian peoples. But some may ask whether it is appropriate to stop the story of liberation at Exodus 14, with the Hebrew slaves crossing the Red Sea and entering the wilderness. For them the events that follow — the song of liberation centred on the mighty acts of Yahweh (Exodus 15) and the covenant on Mount Sinai (Exodus 19ff.) — are equally significant. It was through the covenant that the Israelites realized in a remarkable way that they were people of God not simply because they had been suffering slaves in Egypt but because God chose them for a purpose. Being people of God is not only a privilege but also a responsibility: they were expected to be a blessing for and witness among all nations by obeying God's commandments and establishing a community based on justice, love and peace.

Jesus was a Jew and his early followers were also Jews. They did not ridicule the claim of their Jewish contemporaries to be the descendants of the people of God or the children of Abraham. However, there were moments of confrontation between the Jesus movement and the most conservative wing of the Jewish leadership. To those who boasted that "Abraham is our father" Jesus is reported to have declared, "You are from your father the devil" (John 8:39,44). John the Baptist said to those Jews who came to be baptized by him, "Do not begin to say to yourselves, 'We have Abraham as our ancestor'; for I tell you, God is able from these stones to raise up children to Abraham" (Luke 3:8). Stones here denote insignificant people in the society. It is in this light that we have to understand Jesus' declaring certain types of people to be the children of Abraham — those who were for various reasons alienated in their own society. For example, a woman with 18 years of infirmity, physically and sexually alienated, was called the daughter of Abraham (Luke 13:16).

In the parable of the rich man and Lazarus, the latter, economically alienated, is taken to the bosom of Abraham (Luke 16:22). Zacchaeus, a tax collector who was socially alienated because of his profession, was called a son of Abraham (Luke 19:9). Meeting a centurion who demonstrated greater faith than anyone he had seen from within the Abrahamic fold, Jesus said that "many will come from east and west and sit at table with Abraham" (Matt. 8:11).

The early Christians extended this openness to the Gentiles who came to belong to Christ, calling them "Abraham's offspring, heirs according to the promise" (Gal. 3:29). This new identity as people of God brought a new kind of religious experience, described in the biblical term as "life in Christ", and laid on them a new responsibility of meeting the high ethical standards of a new life.

While Asian theologians hasten to relate Christ to the suffering people of Asia who are for them the people of God, they do not explain the nature of this new life. However, indiscriminately extending the status of people of God to persons of different religions in Asia and rating their religiousness as a source of revelation is problematic. First of all, different religious communities want to define themselves in categories of their own, such as the "enlightened ones" in the case of Buddhists, or followers of an eternal system (*Sanatana Dharma*) in the case of many Hindus. One group of Hindus rejected the name "people of God" when it was imposed on them, as we shall see. In the second place, certain strands of a religion may legitimize and perpetuate social discrimination and oppression. For example, brahminic Hinduism developed the caste system with religious sanction and support. And the Hindu belief of one birth affecting the life of following births is often seen as a hindrance to working for change in conditions of poverty and oppression.

Therefore it is a superficial imposition indiscriminately to call people of different religious and ethnic groups people of God. This is of course not to deny that liberative elements are found in varying degrees in different religious traditions. But it is probably no exaggeration to say that no religious community has preserved the religious significance of its story of oppression and liberation more clearly than the Jews. What Jesus, a devout Jew, told the Samaritan woman at the well is to the point here: "We worship what we know, for salvation is from the Jews" (John 4:22). How Christians and other religious communities today should relate to devout Jews is thus an important question.

Concern and complexity

Attributing the status of people of God to the suffering masses of Asia is a bold theological affirmation by Asian Christian thinkers; indeed, no more eloquent expression could be found of their concern for the poor and oppressed. But this concern is not accompanied by sufficient recognition of the complexity of factors that cause suffering. Removal of the external forces of oppression and domination is seen as guaranteeing a community of love and sharing. Is this not too simplistic — even utopian — a vision?

Kim Yong-Bock puts it well: "The systems of injustice operate in complex ways, and shifting combinations. Under them the people suffer double and triple oppression, which ultimately drains their spiritual vitality." But the operation of these systems needs to be identified in different spheres. One sphere which is repeatedly pointed out is Western domination and colonization, subsequently perpetuated in the influence of multinationals. Occasionally one has the impression that such anti-West attitudes (sometimes on the part of thinkers who themselves have ironically drunk deeply from the wells of the West) leads to a kind of cultural jingoism. One can see similar attitudes in those Hindus of India who fight to establish *Hindutva*, which they interpret as cultural nationalism, when in fact it is this very culture which has sanctioned and sanctified the domination of a particular caste over other communities in India. As exploiters with religious and political power, they are in no way better than the white colonizers, as it is popularly recognized. Here we may recall the words of the report of the spies Moses sent to Canaan, which spoke of "a land that devours its inhabitants" (Numbers 13:33). This can, in differing measures, be applied to all Asian countries today.

The untouchables or dalits are the most oppressed people in India. But dalit women are called the dalits of the dalits, since dalit males share all the dominating characteristics of male chauvinism in general. Dalit children are forced to suffer a triple oppression, since they share the suffering of children in common. Again, in a class analysis, those who are the poorest of the poor among the dalits are akin to other such poor people. In short, it is not enough to identify people in terms of their social and economic standing, as there are gender and age factors which contribute to unjust practices.

Ethnic identities are not always laudable. Too much consciousness of ethnic identities has led to sub-caste clashes among lower castes in India, communal riots between the Indian Muslims and Hindus and ethnic conflicts as we see in Sri Lanka. While oppressive forces are ingeniously getting unified, fragmentation among the victims deprives them of their solidarity and strength. V.S. Naipaul's *India: A Million Mutinies Now* succinctly illustrates this. How can the so-called people of God affirm their solidarity around one God as each ethnic or religious group has its own God, gods or goddesses?

It is all too easy for the liberated to become the oppressor, for Moses to become the Pharaoh. There is a challenging lesson in the "rebellion" of Korah and his company against Moses and Aaron. They said to Moses and Aaron, "You have gone too far! All the congregation are holy, every one of them, and the Lord is among them. So why then do you exalt yourselves above the assembly of the Lord?" (Numbers 16:3). They seem to remind Moses of what he had said earlier: "Would that all the Lord's people were prophets, and that the Lord would put his spirit on them!" (Numbers 11:29). This is not simply a struggle for leadership but resistance to the tendencies of domination within the liberated community. The Hebrew prophets repeatedly reminded the people that having once been slaves they should not be involved in promoting oppression and slavery.

In India certain untouchable communities were liberated through the missionary movement. But now they are indifferent to the suffering of present-day untouchable people or even suppress them if given a chance. Asian theologians tend not to acknowledge this common human tendency to oppress and dominate. Perhaps they are concerned not to be seen as subscribing to the traditional doctrine of original sin or to a fundamentalist view of individual piety. But it is important to recognize this tendency to dominate which manifests itself in various ways and shifting combinations. Again the prophetic tradition of the Jewish people, including the Jesus movement, remains distinctive for providing an ongoing self-critical mechanism.

Asian theologians stress that suffering is caused by unjust systems. But there are different perceptions of suffering in Asian religious traditions. Buddhists view suffering as a fundamental character of life caused by desire. For most Vedantins it is due to inherent ignorance of the system and operation of life. There are Hindus who see it as the effect of their actions in their previous lives. Many Christians and Muslims explain it as the will of God operating beyond human comprehension. In any case, it is important to have dialogue with these and other groups and help them to realize how much of the suffering of people today could be avoided by establishing just systems. This is not to ignore the tragedies, natural calamities, overpopulation, disabilities, disease and death that people in various circumstances suffer in their day-to-day life. Systematic analysis may not be immediately relevant and helpful in all cases. Moreover, it is reductionistic to see justice only in terms of impersonal systems of politics and economy. Justice is fundamentally a matter of right relationships, at the heart of which is the willingness of people to share their resources and powers with others.

How can this willingness be created? Battles have been fought in the name of justice, quarrels ignited, feuds promoted. The result is mutual destruction. Protestant Christianity in India, for example, was to a great extent the result of peoples' movements and social libera- tion. But Christians failed to form themselves into a community combining love and mutual give-and-take with their social conscious- ness. Consequently, there is so much of competition and power struggles in the churches that there is hardly any time to think of their mission and witness. When we affirm the transforming power of the Holy Spirit in society, we also have to be on the lookout for the fruits of the Spirit, such as love, kindness and patience.

A similar observation may be applicable to the political scene in Asia. While we extol people's participation in social, economic and political life through the democratic process, we should recognize the limitations of democracy in the way it operates today. As Kim Yong- Bock observes:

> "Democracy" is the most hypocritically used term in the world today, being the tool with which the powers try to legitimize the status quo. Liberal democratic languages are guilty of this misuse. Some liberal democratic politics in Asia, by ensuring the participation of the powerful minority, open the way to freer encroachment by the global economic powers into the socio-economic and cultural life of the people ("AMC Report", p.27).

The powers are not only global but also national, regional and local. This is abundantly evident in India, for example. India is the largest democracy in the world and the first Asian country to adopt social democracy after independence. But how can the benefits of democracy be expected to reach the nearly 50 percent of the people who are illiterate and live below the poverty line? The Indian masses are drawn by glamorous and fascinating propaganda to sacrifice before their political gods and goddesses. Moreover, in a multi-faith and multi-ethnic context, with majorities and minorities of various types and having common civil and criminal laws but different personal laws for different religious communities, Indian secular democracy is repeatedly diverted to serve the dominating powers.

Then what political options and ideological roads lie before the people of God in Asia? Benevolent dictatorships often turn to be malevolent. The experiments of both capitalism and communism have proved to be a failure. Theocracies end up in exclusivism and fundamentalism. The biblical people of God experienced the leadership of heroes, tribal confederation, monarchy and governorship under an imperial power. Finally, they expected a Messiah, an embodiment of justice and love, either in the form of a political ruler or a suffering servant. In Asian reflections, domination is contrasted with "doularchy" — leading by serving — mastery with ministry. Neither the Jewish community nor the Christian community nor any secular community has ever realized and demonstrated fully this counter-structure. While striving towards that, our only possible option is to watch political developments carefully and to play a prophetic role.

In this connection, the ethical imperative of our religious vision can no longer be presented through a complicated system of doctrines and laws. Rather its essence has to be presented in summary form. We have biblical insights to do so. For example, the prophet Micah writes: "He has told you, O mortal, what is good; and what does the Lord require of you but to do justice, and to love kindness, and to walk humbly with your God?" (Micah 6:8). The parallel Christian summary, repeatedly mentioned in the New Testament, is "Love one another" (cf. 1 John 4:7). It may be expected that people of other faiths will come up with their own summaries in a similar way, as Gandhi projected non-violence as the essence of Hinduism, Buddhist compassion, Muslim brotherhood, Sikh equality and so on. These are points of contact for creative dialogue among people of different faiths on the meaning of life and on creating a just world.

Beyond the category "people of God"

The Jewish people are unique in defining themselves as the people of God in the sense of a people chosen for a universal purpose. God said "my people" for the first time when he saw the affliction of the Israelites in Egypt (Exodus 3:7). In the background was his remembrance of his covenant with their ancestors (Exodus 2:24; 3:6). But God made a new covenant with the Israelites in the wilderness which gave them the special status of not only "a people" but also "God's own possession, a priestly kingdom and a holy nation" (Exodus 19:6). The only condition was "if you obey my voice and keep my covenant" (v.5). Such expectations of his people in the world on God's part could lead to their punishment (Amos 3:2) and even the threat of God's saying that they were *not* his people (Hosea 1:9). Thus the status of people of God had to be kept in dialectic tension.

As Jewish people, the early Christians were aware of this tension. However, they defined themselves as people of God, a chosen race, royal priesthood and a holy nation (1 Peter 2:9; Revelation 5:10). The basis was a new covenant made through the blood of Christ, which was inclusive, welcoming the Gentiles into it. Those who were "aliens from the commonwealth of Israel" and "no people" became people of God (Ephesians 2:12; 1 Peter 2:10). They were given the Aaronic blessing of Yahweh plus the Pauline blessing of Trinity.

We have suggested above that it is an imposition to identify as "people of God" those from different religious communities who want to define themselves in their own way. This is illustrated by an Indian example. Gandhi chose to call the untouchables "people of God" — *Harijans*. But the people themselves rejected this term. *Hari* signifies the brahminic god Vishnu, even if Gandhi tried to interpret it as a common name for God. Thus the new name *Harijan* provided no escape from the age-old curse of untouchability. Better to call the wrong by its own name, so that the wrongdoer will feel the need of redressing it, than to conceal the reality and give false absolution. There was a feeling that the new name reflected pity on the part of tyrants who wanted to exploit their helplessness and dependency.

Some were aware of the connotation of "people of God" as children born through temple prostitution. Hence the untouchable people themselves chose the name *dalit*, meaning "broken", to define themselves and struggle for their rights. Similar problems with the term "people of God" would no doubt be expressed by other religious and ethnic communities.

It is also worth noting that "people of God" was only one of many categories which the early Christians used to define themselves. Other categories are more common and universal. For example, Paul speaks of "one new humanity" created in Christ's breaking down the dividing wall of hostility (Ephesians 2:15). Elsewhere he writes: "There is no longer Jew or Greek, there is no longer slave or free, there is no longer male and female; for all of you are *one in Christ Jesus*" (Galatians 3:28). This one new humanity extends to embrace all people in all places. That is why such Indian Christian thinkers as P.D. Devanandan and M.M. Thomas have highlighted "new creation", "one humanity" and "humanization" as key categories for theological reflection.

If the terms "humanity" and "new creation" sound abstract, one New Testament alternative is "children of God" (Romans 8:16). These are persons who are born again, taking a new orientation in life (John 3:3-8). Jesus asked adults to look at children as recipients of the kingdom of God, displaying its life-style and indicating the quality of a new leadership. "Children" not only signifies those who are young and tender in age and development but also those who are weak and vulnerable, as the Bible makes amply evident. Recognizing the presence of age bias in theology and undialogical rigidity and stubbornness in adult theologians, some have proposed children as a key category for a creative theology, involving a new spirituality, a new theological approach calling all people to become childlike and a new understanding of growth as the dynamic cycle of being born again and again and growing up to salvation (cf. 1 Peter 2:2). Age and long tradition do not matter much. If the Jewish people claim to be the "first-born", there are thousands today who may claim to be "new-born". Some Christian converts in India have, with their poetic imagination, identified themselves as children newly adopted or newly born.

Finally, a vision for the future of humanity is integral to our understanding of the people of God. Since religions differ widely in this respect, we confine ourselves here to the vision of the Jews and Christians. Of many aspects of the Jewish vision, the early Christians affirmed the expectation of a new heaven and new earth (Isaiah 65:17; Revelation 21:1). They also set the goal of not only attaining "maturity, to the measure of the full stature of Christ" (Ephesians 4:13), but of being "filled with all the fullness of God" (Ephesians 3:19). It was the Jewish Jesus who said, "Be perfect, therefore, as your heavenly Father is perfect" (Matthew 5:48). One clue to this perfection is God's making his sun to rise on the evil and on the good, and sending rain on the just and on the unjust (v.45). Those who define the suffering masses of Asia as people of God but cannot define the oppressors in similar terms nor identify them exactly in the shifting combinations of injustice will find it difficult to understand perfection in this way.

What is possible now, however, is to call all people to repentance, a turning around and a new orientation in life, whose implications would of course differ from person to person. It is a humbling thought that no other religious community has a mandate for calling people to repent or to turn to God such as Jews and Christians do. Christians will make this call in the name of Jesus, believing that he was made by God to be Christ, Lord and Saviour. All things are to be subjected under his feet because he remains standing and slain, dead and risen, persuading and serving. All people and all things are safe with this figure of crucified power.

Ultimately, "when all things are subjected to him, then the Son himself will also be subjected to the one who put all things in subjection under him, so that God may be all in all" (1 Corinthians 15:28). This vision provides sufficient impetus for Jews and Christians to work together for a "process of peopling" or making many to be people or children of God, while they continue in dialogue with people of other faiths.

NOTES

[1] Steven G. Mackie, "God's People in Asia: A Key Concept in Asian Theology", *Scottish Journal of Theology*, vol. 42, nos 1-4, 1989, pp.215-40.
[2] *Peoples of Asia, People of God*, Hong Kong, Christian Conference of Asia, 1990.

IV

Attitudes to
Religious Diversity

9. Faith in the Midst of Faiths: Traditional Jewish Attitudes

NORMAN SOLOMON

That neither the Jewish nor the Christian faith is dominant in Asia does not mean that we lack the ambition or at least the hope that our faith will "triumph" in the end; but our minority status predisposes us to theologies which play down the triumphalist aspects of our heritage — a way in which many contemporary Asian Christian theologians differ notably from the Christian missionaries who introduced the "imperial" religion to Asia.

This paper explores the Jewish sources of Judaism, biblical and rabbinic, to discover those elements on which a pluralist rather than a triumphalist theology can be built today. In this process of selection I have allowed myself to be influenced by those values which are often today referred to as "enlightened" or "humanitarian" values, which the liberal democratic societies of the West love to claim as their own. But the distinction between traditional religious values and humanitarian values is not clear-cut. It is legitimate to view so-called humanitarian values as themselves arising out of traditional faith. Certainly the shrill accusation that there is some sharp dichotomy between "Western values" and those of Judaism, Christianity and Islam is tendentious; and some of the common generalizations about differences between "East" and "West" are equally fatuous.

A first reading of either our common Hebrew scripture or the New Testament would seem to deny that there is any room for plurality, at least in religious faith. Of course, human natures are diverse and peoples are diverse one from another; and it is readily acknowledged that such diversity contributes to the greater glory of God. But religious faith is another matter. Deuteronomy thunders against the idolaters, "You shall break down their altars, and dash in pieces their pillars, and hew down their Asherim, and burn their graven images with fire" (7:5). In the New Testament the gospel of John declares "none shall come to the Father but through me"; and the book of Revelation reveals the torment and eternal damnation of the unbelievers. This hardly seems fertile ground for a pluralistic world in which people of different faiths can coexist in mutual respect and love.

History points the same way. Too often when religious leaders hold sway over government, whether by usurping power or by influencing the rulers, diversity is thwarted — not only the diversity of faiths, but diversity within each faith. In the great wars of religion of 16th-century Europe, Christian princes wrought havoc on the Christian people in misguided and ultimately abortive attempts to stamp out diversity and establish one universal church.

One can well understand the humanists who, seeking to assert the richness of diversity, turn their backs on tradition. But tradition is more complex than they allow. In reviewing the sources of the Jewish tradition I shall not conceal those elements which have tended to smother diversity; at the same time, I shall draw special attention to those elements which can help us to welcome wholeheartedly the full miscellany of human experience and expression.

The celebration of diversity

Some forms of diversity are consistently celebrated, both in scripture and in the rabbinic literature.

Diversity in creation. Genesis celebrates each species of plant and animal created *l'minehu* — according to its own kind. In the book of Psalms, in Job and elsewhere, the rich diversity of nature is portrayed as witness to the glory of God its creator.

Diversity of human personality. Moses, appealing to God to appoint a successor, addresses him as *Elohei ha-ruhot l'khol basar*, "God of the spirits of all flesh" (Numbers 27:16; cf. 16:22), the God who knows, understands, values each individual human soul. Witnesses in capital cases are sternly reminded of God's greatness as creator of diverse human personalities:

> Humankind was produced from one individual, Adam... to show God's greatness. When a man mints coins in a press, each is identical; but when the king of kings of kings, the holy one, blessed be he, creates people in the form of Adam not one is similar to any other (Mishna *Sanhedrin* 4:5).

In the same vein, one who sees 600,000 of Israel should bless "him who is the master of secrets" — the God who knows and values each individual. A popular midrashic explanation of the four plants waved on the festival of Succot is that they symbolize four categories of people (variously defined, but always including "marginals") who must come together in praise of God; and a public fast of intercession which lacks the participation of sinners is declared no fast.

Diversity of nations is further evidence of God's greatness, at least when they join in his praise: "From the rising of the sun to its setting the name of the Lord is to be praised" (Psalm 113:3).

But therein lies the rub. The diversity of nations is indeed glorious, but only when they praise God — *our* God. The one form of diversity that is rejected is diversity of faith. God is a "jealous God", and there is room for no other beside him.

So we must go on to examine biblical and later attitudes to "other faiths", and assess whether it is possible after all to introduce something of the traditional affirmation of the value of diversity even into the sacred realm of faith.

The biblical attitude to other faiths

Three leading concepts on "other people" underlie much of the Hebrew scriptures: (1) universality, the certainty that God's concern is for all people; (2) non-exclusiveness, the idea that knowledge of God is neither exclusive, limited to Israel, nor esoteric, limited to initiates; (3) boundaries, a strong line of demarcation between right and wrong, true and false, holy and profane, those who follow God and idolaters — distinctions which tend to be confused with that between Israel and the nations.

Universality

Genesis not only stresses the unity of humankind but even shows God trying first, through Adam, to relate to humankind as a whole. Israel is eventually chosen not for its own sake but for his mission. God never loses sight, so to speak, of the fact that Israel is his means of impressing the nations. When God threatens to destroy Israel and to make Moses into "a great nation" (Exodus 32:7ff.), Moses dares to appeal to God's concern for public relations. What impression would such a deed make on the Egyptians, whom God surely wants to win over by demonstrating his care and power? When Solomon dedicates the temple, he sees it as a religious centre for all humankind; in no way does he see Jerusalem as a political capital from which Israel will dominate the nations, but as a spiritual centre through which they will draw inspiration (1 Kings 8). The shortest of all the Psalms crystallizes this thought:

> Praise the Lord, all nations,
> extol him all you peoples;
> for his love protecting us is strong,
> the Lord's constancy is everlasting (Psalm 117, NEB).

The *goyim*, the "nations" or "Gentiles", should learn about God not through conquest by Israel but through grateful and admiring acknowledgment of what God has done for Israel. When Isaiah says, "You are my witnesses" (43:10), the reference is not to the people's suffering, not even to their virtuous life, but to the great things God is seen to do for them.

Non-exclusiveness

Scripture recognizes and appreciates that God is "known" by people other than Israel. These may be independent individuals like Melchizedek (Genesis 14:18) or persons like Jethro (Exodus 18) or Naaman (2 Kings 5) who are impressed by particular acts of God. In later times there is a glowing satisfaction that the nations are getting to know God: "From the rising of the sun to its setting the name of the Lord is to be praised" (Psalm 113:3; other interpretations are possible).

An individual may, of course, like Ruth, be adopted into Israel; but this is neither required nor expected. The fulfilment of Israel's mission is not that all other people become Israel, but that each nation, remaining what it is — Egyptian, Assyrian or whatever — pay homage to God and be guided by his will. The nations are expected to remain ethnically and culturally distinct, while cleansing themselves of idolatry.

Demarcation

The acceptance of the idea that other nations too are cared for by God (Amos 9:7 contra Amos 3:2) and are part of his ultimate plan for the world does not carry the corollary that idolatry, their normal form of worship, is acceptable. True, Yehezkel Kaufmann, in his monumental study of the religion of Israel, contends that according to the Bible only Israel was forbidden to worship idols. [1] Philo and Josephus, as well as more recent Jewish apologists, have argued on this basis for tolerance of "pagan" religions, [2] even though the alleged destruction of temples in Cyrene during the "Revolt of the Diaspora" under Trajan (116-17 C.E.) suggests that some Jews took an opposite view. Undoubtedly, the rabbis distinguished in this respect between the land of Israel, where no idolatry was to be tolerated, and the lands outside, where Gentiles should not be disturbed in their worship. [3] But even if Kaufmann was right, this would merely show that God was prepared to put up with idolaters for a bit longer, not that his ultimate design was that any people should continue to worship idols. Kaufmann pointed out that the Hebrew scriptures are to a very considerable extent a polemic against idolatry, showing neither interest in nor understanding of a "deeper level" in what it castigates as mere "worship of sticks and stones".

In the context of Asian religions and cultures, this poses an acute problem for Jews and Christians. Is it honest, let alone ethical, to represent the dominant religions of Asia as "worship of sticks and stones"? Are we not bearing false witness against Hindus, Buddhists and others who would with ample justification categorically reject and resent such a characterization of their faiths? We may not feel comfortable with worship directed to or through images, but neither can we feel comfortable with the biblical equation of idolatry with immorality.

Still, scripture does emphatically draw boundaries:

> You shall not make yourselves vile through beast or bird or anything that creeps on the ground, for I have made a clear separation between them and you, declaring them unclean. You shall be holy to me, because I the Lord am holy. I have made a clear separation between you and the heathen, that you may belong to me (Leviticus 20:25-7).

How do we interpret those boundaries? Are they drawn between those who worship through images and those who do not? Scripture itself always justifies the boundary before idolatry in terms of either a further ethical or moral boundary or a rejection of the literal belief that the image worshipped has power to "save". Neither of these arguments supports a wholesale rejection of Hinduism or Buddhism, the former because many Hindus and Buddhists are people of high ethical and moral standards, the latter because the simplistic type of belief in idols portrayed in Scripture does not correspond with the reality of Hindu and Buddhist teaching; and if it is alleged that popular Hinduism and Buddhism conform to the biblical stereotype of idolatry, no less could be said of popular expressions of Christianity in many parts of the world. A faith is not to be judged by the popular superstition which surrounds it.

Talmud

Sheva mitzvot

The rabbis list seven commandments as incumbent upon the "children of Noah", that is, people other than Israel. The earliest version of this list is found in the Tosefta, a rabbinic work largely redacted in the third century:

> The children of Noah were given seven commandments: laws [i.e., to establish courts of justice], [prohibition of] idolatry, blasphemy, sexual immorality, bloodshed, theft and the limb from a living animal [certain types of cruelty to animals?] (Tosefta *Avoda Zara* 9:4).

Rabbinic comment anchors these commandments in Scripture, particularly Genesis 9.

These seven laws constitute an attempt to formulate moral standards for the world without a concomitant demand for conversion or submission to Israel. As such, they represent one of the most remarkable initiatives in the history of the monotheistic religions, for they acknowledge the right of peoples to their own formulation of faith, provided only that a minimum, almost "humanistic" standard of behaviour is met.

Occasionally scholars summarizing the *sheva mitzvot*, include "belief in God". This is a careless misrepresentation of the prohibition of either idolatry or blasphemy. Not one of the early versions of the *sheva mitzvot* lists "belief in God". The rabbis were far more concerned with the rejection of idolatry than with the formulation of "definitions" of God. An express demand for belief in God would have required some understanding, some definition of God; and this was precisely the area into which the rabbis did not wish to enter. They asked only that the worship of idols cease and the worship of God be taken seriously and treated with respect; there was to be no emphasis on the substantive content of belief in God. Assertions *about* God did not matter, holiness of life did. In complete conformity with this view the third-century Palestinian R. Yohanan declared: "Whoever denies idolatry is called *yehudi* [a Jew]".[4] It is the rejection of idolatry and respect for God-talk and worship, not recognition of a pre-defined divine being, which is the foundation of Noahide law as conceived by the rabbis.

The concept of the *sheva mitzvot* is a powerful model for contemporary theologians seeking a basis for the affirmation of "other faiths".

One might have expected that the Noahide laws would become the basis of and stimulus for an active Jewish mission towards the Gentiles, for these laws were designed to express the Torah's minimum standards for non-Jews. However, the date of their formulation in the third century coincided with an increase in "straight" proselytizing by Jews, and once proselytizing was made virtually impossible under Christian rule it was no longer realistic to proselytize even on a Noahide basis.

In modern times there have been some attempts to revive the concept. The cabbalist rabbi Elia Benamozegh of Leghorn (1823-1900) persuaded a Catholic would-be convert to Judaism, Aimé Pallière, to adopt Noahism rather than full-blown Judaism. Although Pallière championed Noahism until the end of his life in 1949, he attracted interest rather than followers.[5] Aaron Lichtenstein, who has documented more recent Noahism, observes that "the worst hardship borne by practising Noahites is the lack of fellowship". Nevertheless, the movement has grown and now numbers several thousand individuals. The journal *The Gap* is published in Athens, Tennessee (USA), where they hold an annual international congress.

Closer to the mainstream of Jewish religious activity is the impetus the *sheva mitzvot* concept gives to Jews to accept moral responsibility in society in general, for it demands that support and encouragement be given to "the nations" to uphold at least this standard. A notable instance of this was a series of public addresses and interventions by the Hasidic leader Menahem Mendel Schneersohn (the "Lubavitcher Rebbe") of New York, expounding the Noahide laws in relation to the needs of contemporary society. This included an exchange of letters with US President Ronald Reagan in 1986 in which Schneersohn commends the president for "giving valuable support to the dissemination of the Seven Noahide Laws, so basic to any society worthy of its name". While this exchange was politically naive, it does seem to me important as a model for a religious input to society uncompromised by conversionist overtones.

In the second century Rabbi Joshua ben Hananya propounded the view, later generally accepted, that "the righteous of all nations have a share in the world to come" (Tosefta *Sanhedrin* 13), though they were not converted to Judaism. There is no equivalent in Judaism to Cyprian's *extra ecclesiam nulla salus* ("no salvation outside the church"). The concept of "righteous Gentiles" provides a further basis for the affirmation of the spiritual worth of individuals of other faiths.

Discriminatory and anti-social legislation

The "demarcation" aspect of rabbinic Judaism is most clearly evidenced by the lengthy history of rules, particularly regarding food, idolatry and ritual purity, devised by the rabbis and their predecessors to separate Jews from the heathen environment — and occasionally even from Jews who were less devout brethren. Parallels to this can be found in developments within the early church and other religious communities.

Moreover, rabbinic hermeneutics often limited the operation of biblical rules to the faithful among the people of Israel, leaving them the problem of how such basic ideas as respect for proprietary rights and regard for human dignity apply to non-Israelites. Their solution was to formulate a series of broad principles such as *tiqqun 'olam* ("establishing the world aright"), *darkhe shalom* ("the ways of peace") and *qiddush Hashem* ("sanctifying God's name", that is, behaving in a way that brings credit to God). Among other things, these principles serve to govern the relationships of Jews to those outside the bond of faith or peoplehood. They afford a basis for what Hans Küng has called a *Weltethos* (global ethic), which though well rooted within Jewish tradition is not tied to its specific doctrines and rituals.

Interfaith relations: four rabbinic models

Mediaeval Jewish thinkers, unlike their forbears in late antiquity, were often aware of what Christians and Muslims actually taught and believed, and offered comment, whether by way of defence or instruction. Sometimes this is found in the context of "disputation", which frequently elicited from Jews some of their best apologetic. There is, however, a serious difficulty in reconciling the philosophical reflections on other faiths with the assumptions which seem to be made by those who develop the law.

1. Other religions as idolatry

The first traditional Jewish model for relating to other religions is negative. Muslims and Christians are idolaters, with perhaps the qualification that they are not necessarily idolaters in the full biblical sense, but *maase avotehem bidehem* — they continue through inertia inherited patterns of idolatrous worship.[6]

The lines of boundary, of demarcation, were indeed strongly drawn in the Middle Ages. Jews lived in autonomous communities, and were regarded as a "people apart". For their part, Jews adhered to the old rabbinic laws which had been designed specifically to separate them from pagans. Jacob Katz has documented what he regards as the relaxation of those laws, particularly in Christian countries, in the Middle Ages.[7] Indeed, the mediaeval halakhists were often less stringent in applying the laws of idolatry, wine and interest than the rabbis of the Talmud had been. However, I cannot accept Katz's contention that this was a consequence of a more tolerant attitude towards the Christian faith; rather, the new theological assessment of Christian teaching was invoked in justification of established customary practice in Western lands.

What is interesting is the disjunction between law and theology. Laws continued — and still continue — to define orthodox practice, even though the "theology" on which they were originally based is no longer applicable. It would be a mistake to argue that because the law continued to be expressed in the same forms as when the surrounding nations were all pagan, it meant that Jews regarded Christians and Muslims as pagans. The law has actually become detached from its origins, and the theological status within Judaism of Christians and Muslims is defined quite differently from their juridical status. In a situation of power, this tension would have to be resolved; but until recently Jews have not collectively been in a situation of power.

2. Islam and Christianity as preparing the way

The second model is hinted at by Sa'adia al-Fayyumi (882-942) and more fully developed by Judah Halevi (c. 1075-1141) and Moses Maimonides (1135-1204). Islam and Christianity are in error, but can be accommodated as part of the divine design to bring the nations gradually to God. The other monotheistic religions, says Halevi, "serve to introduce and pave the way for the expected Messiah, who is the fruition, and they will all become his fruit". [8]

In a paragraph censored from the printed editions of the Mishneh Torah, Maimonides rejects the truth-claims of Christianity and Islam on the basis that they fail to meet the criterion of consistency with the Torah of Moses. Despite this, he assigns both Christianity and Islam a role in the process of world redemption:

> The teachings of him of Nazareth [Jesus] and of the man of Ishmael [Muhammad] who arose after him help to bring all mankind to perfection, so that they may serve God with one consent. For insofar as the whole world is full of talk of the Messiah, of words of Holy Writ and of the Commandments — these words have spread to the ends of the earth, even if many deny their binding character at the present time. When the Messiah comes all will return from their errors.

3. Menahem ha-Meiri and theistic morality

The Provençal rabbi Menahem ha-Meiri (d. c. 1315), anxious to avoid identification of people of other religions in his own time with pagan idolaters, coined the phrase *umot hagedurot bedarkei hadatot* ("nations bound by the ways of religion") to justify what was probably already a customary relaxation of certain rabbinic laws. In effect, he made possible a still more positive assessment of the way of life, if not the doctrines, of Christians. [9]

4. Nethanel ibn Fayyumi: each nation has its own prophet

The fourth model is that described by the Yemenite Jewish philosopher Nethanel ibn Fayyumi (d. c. 1164). If we take Nethanel's words at face value, he asserts the authenticity of the prophecy of Muhammad, as revealed in the Quran, and at least the possibility that there are additional authentic revelations (he does not mention Christianity).

Let us follow the steps by which Nethanel reaches his contention that the prophecy of Muhammad is authentic: [10]

> The first creation of God was the universal intellect... Its exuberant joy and happiness caused an overflow, and thus there emanated from it the universal soul (2,94)...
>
> Through the necessity of his wisdom... he mercifully vouchsafed unto mortals a revelation from the holy world — the world of the universal soul — which originated from the overflow of its holy cause, the universal intellect — which in turn goes back to its originator — may he be exalted! This... expressed itself in an individual man whose spirit is free from the impurity of nature and is disciplined in the noblest science and the purest works... [a] prophet (2,95).
>
> Know then... nothing prevents God from sending into his world whomsoever he wishes, since the world of holiness sends forth emanations unceasingly... Even before the revelation of the law he sent prophets to the nations... and again after its revelation nothing prevented him from sending to them whom he wishes so that the world might not remain without religion (103f.)...
>
> Mohammed was a prophet to them but not to those who preceded [i.e., were prior to] them in the knowledge of God [i.e., older = better] (105)...
>
> He permitted to every people something he forbade to others (107)... He sends a prophet to every people according to their language (109).

Nethanel interprets revelation in a "naturalistic" fashion. It is a universal phenomenon, of which Muhammad is a specific instance. He parallels his philosophical arguments with a skilful use of Jewish midrashic material.

Nethanel's position differs radically from the popular and more traditional attitude of such as Maimonides, whose vigorous defence of the monotheistic purity of Islam was matched by an equally vigorous denial of the authenticity of its prophet. Nethanel is neither casual nor tongue-in-cheek in his assessment of Muhammad, but presents the reader with a fully integrated system of thought which allows a measure of religious pluralism. The statement about Muhammad is in no way detached from the rest of his thought; it is a key statement within an extensively elaborated philosophical system which carries the social implication of respect for the heirs of the prophets, these heirs being the "imams, administrators, the learned and the wise" (51).

Of these four models, Nethanel's philosophy clearly offers by far the soundest basis for a modern approach to the plurality of faiths.

The Enlightenment

The Enlightenment stressed universal human values and reason rather than creeds, posing a challenge to the conventional Christian view. This new orientation was welcomed by a small number of 18th-century Jews, mainly German, who were sufficiently emancipated to share in contemporary intellectual development. The Swiss deacon Johann Caspar Lavater publicly challenged Moses Mendelssohn (1729-1786) either to refute Christianity or to do what "reason and integrity would otherwise lead him to do" — become a Christian. In a courageous reply Mendelssohn strongly affirmed his faith in Judaism, and even claimed superiority for that faith on the ground that it is fundamentally more tolerant than Christianity:

> According to the basic principles of my religion I am not to seek to convert anyone not born into our laws... Our rabbis unanimously teach that the written and oral laws which comprise our revealed religion are obligatory upon our nation only... We believe the other nations of the earth are directed by God to observe [only] the law of nature and the religion of the Patriarchs. Those who conduct their lives in accordance with this religion of nature and reason are known as *Hasidei Umot ha-Olam*, "righteous Gentiles", and are "children of everlasting salvation". So far are our rabbis from wishing to convert that they instruct us to dissuade, by earnest remonstrance, any who come forward of their own accord...
>
> If, amongst my contemporaries, there were a Confucius or a Solon, I could, consistently with my religious principles, love and admire the great man; the ridiculous thought of converting Confucius or Solon would not enter my head. Convert him indeed! Why? He is not of the Congregation of Jacob, and therefore not subject to my religious laws... Do I think he would be "saved"? I fancy that whosoever leads men to virtue in this life cannot be damned in the next...

Mendelssohn was not unaware that some of the early rabbis had taken a more outgoing attitude towards conversion, but he seems to have underestimated it or else to have played it down for apologetic

reasons. His "religion of nature and reason" is clearly an Enlightenment version of the Noahide commandments. As Katz writes, "Mendelssohn based his predictions upon the assumption that there would
come about a complete severance between church and state, i.e.
between the institutions of religion and of government."[11]

What is important here is not so much Mendelssohn's interpretation of Judaism, though its powerful influence on later Jewish
apologetic is readily acknowledged. It is rather that Mendelssohn so
clearly recognizes the *political* aspects of the problem. Mendelssohn
poses, to an ostensibly Christian state, the question of how it will treat
its citizens, even of whom it will recognize as citizens. His answer is
that *all* must be equal before the law of the state.

Whether this is compatible with Christian, Muslim or Jewish
religious tradition is arguable. In modern times, it has come to be
accepted as the norm within Christian lands. It is a major issue in
Muslim countries; and India has recently seen its democratic, pluralist
traditions undermined by the ominous rise of Hindu nationalism. In
principle, at least, Israel guarantees equality before the law to all,
though several problems need to be solved, including those posed by
the Law of Return and by the status of non-Orthodox Jews.

* * *

Here, with Mendelssohn, lies the sharp end of our consideration of
religious plurality. Unless cordiality, friendship, mutual affirmation
can be translated into human rights, including uncompromised equality before the law, without regard to race, colour, gender or religion,
we are paying mere lip service to a beautiful idea.

Those of us who value our identity as Jews, Christians or Muslims
are challenged to reassess our traditions in the light of important
differences between our contemporary world and the world in which
our faiths were classically formulated, such as:

— Our concept of the world and its nature and "purpose" has been
  radically changed by scientific discoveries from Copernicus onwards.
— Philosophers have forced us to revise our notions of truth and its
  relationship to the way we use language.

— Improved communications — in the understanding of language and literature, as well as in physical mobility and through radio and electronics — rule out cultural and religious isolation as an option.
— Greater firepower and the historical demonstration that technological progress does not automatically reduce conflicts make necessary a global approach to the achievement of peace, comprising all nations irrespective of their religions.
— Conservation of the planet and its resources demands global commitment and organization. We share the planet with each other or else we all perish.

From our survey of Jewish sources, I would highlight the following as potentially the most apt principles on which to found an affirmation of the value of diversity, even in the sacred field of faith.

1. The universalism which is present from scripture onwards must continue to be a cornerstone of Jewish thought. It must be kept in permanent tension with just as much of particularism as is necessary to maintain self-identity.

2. The Noahide commandments offer a framework which embraces the whole world within Torah, yet does not seek to impose distinctive Jewish practice and doctrines. It does indeed allow a special position to "Israel" (not the State of Israel, but rather the Jewish people as party to a special covenant with God). But why should other peoples not understand themselves in the same way? The Noahide system could be looked on as a prototype for each and every ethnic, national or religious group, which will wish to maintain its distinctiveness under a broad universalist umbrella. [12] This is akin to the concept of "local theologies", well known among Asian Christians and now recognized by most churches as a proper and legitimate expression of Christian faith which in no way contradicts its universal character.

3. A "global ethic", independent of the restricted system of halakha and of specific elements of Jewish theology, arises naturally from the series of broad principles including *tiqqun 'olam*, *darkhe shalom* and *qiddush Hashem*, used by the rabbis to govern the relationships of Jews to those outside the bond of faith or peoplehood.

4. The philosophy of Nethanel ibn Fayyumi offers a model, until now ignored by Jewish thinkers, for a concept of universal revelation.

The assertion of the full authenticity of one prophetic revelation does not, for Nethanel, imply the denial of authenticity of other revelations even where there are apparent contradictions between them.

5. The diversities of creation, of individual personalities and of nations have been celebrated from scriptural times onwards. We must extend this celebration to the sphere of faith, recognizing that God is glorified not only in the number of people who praise him in a specific way, but in the variety of ways in which he is perceived and the variety of language and ritual in which he is approached.

It is clear that a palette of resources exists within Jewish tradition to justify the confident affirmation of the plurality of religious expression. This diversity is to be cherished as testimony to the glory of God, who is too great to be contained in one tradition or reserved for one people. This affirmation of the value of diversity must be implemented in our social structures, so that every vestige of discrimination on grounds of colour, gender, race and religion disappears from our constitutions, law codes and ways of life.

NOTES

[1] Yehezkel Kaufmann, *Toldot ha-Emunah ha-Israelit*, 4 vols, Tel Aviv, 1948ff., tr. and abridged by M. Greenberg, *The Religion of Israel*, Chicago, Univ. of Chicago Press, 1960

[2] Philo of Alexandria, *De Specialibus Legibus* 1:53 (Loeb edition, VII, 128); Josephus *Antiquities* IV.viii.10 (Loeb edition, IV, 207), cf. *Against Apion* II.144. More recently, J.H. Hertz, *The Pentateuch and Haftorahs*, London, Soncino Press, 1960, p.759, commenting on Deuteronomy 4:19, suggests that the words "which he apportioned to them" indicate a biblical recognition that it is acceptable for the nations to worship their own gods. This is disingenuous.

[3] E.g. Babylonian Talmud *Hullin* 13b and Talmud Yerushalmi *Berakhot* 9:2. Of course, this does not imply that the rabbis did not expect that idolatry would eventually be uprooted from the whole world; cf. *Tosefta Berakhot* 6:2.

[4] Babylonian Talmud *Megilla* 13a.

[5] E. Benamozegh, *Israele e l'Umanità*, tr. Marco Morselli, Genoa, Casa Editrice Marietti, 1990.

[6] Babylonian Talmud *Hullin* 13b.

[7] Jacob Katz, *Exclusiveness and Tolerance*, London, Oxford U.P., 1961, ch.10.

[8] Judah Halevi, *The Kuzari*, tr. Hartwig Hirschfeld, New York, Schocken, 1964, V, 3.

[9] Jacob Katz, *loc. cit.*

[10] References are to the translation by D. Levine, *The Garden of Wisdom*, New York, Columbia U.P., 1907, (repr. 1966). The best and most recent edition of the Judaeo-Arabic text, with a Hebrew translation and notes, is Y. Kafih, *Bustan el-Uqul: Gan ha-Sekhalim*, Jerusalem, Halikhot Am Israel, 1984.

[11] Jacob Katz, *loc. cit.*

[12] David Hartman develops the theme of the two covenants — that of creation and that of Sinai — in *Conflicting Visions*, New York, Schocken Books, 1990, pp.246-65. The creation covenant is universal and for all time; the Sinai covenant with Israel does not preclude parallel covenants with other societies. This allows for a plurality of revelations, each God's way of speaking to a particular group of people. Islam and Christianity would hold an equal place with numerous other "covenant" societies. Such an approach is close to that of ibn Fayyumi.

10. An Indian Christian View of Religious Pluralism

ISRAEL SELVANAYAGAM

"God is one; you call him (or her) Yahweh, Mary or Jesus Christ; Muslims call him Allah and Sikhs Sat Nam; we call him Krishna, Rama, Siva, Kali and so on. You have a temple and priests, the practice of giving offerings, the sharing of sacred food — as we also have. You try to get your soul into eternal rest, as we do. Our ways may be different, but the goal is the same."

Over the past seventeen years this has been the typical response to religious pluralism from the average Hindu I have met in my ministry of inter-religious dialogue. It is a frustrating response for two reasons. First, my Hindu partners in dialogue are not able to see their own faith and other faiths distinctively. Second, the Christian faith has been presented to them in such a way that they do not see anything new. What then should be my response in this situation?

Christians, along with many Jews and Muslims, believe in one God, the only creator of the world and of all people. But Christians also believe in Jesus Christ, and hold that his life, death and resurrection have a universal significance. We believe in the Holy Spirit, a Christian fellowship, divine judgment and eternal life. Because of these affirmations we may appear to be "exclusive", but there is in fact no reason to identify Christianity with being triumphalistic, arrogant or socially excluding. As we believe that God is one, our effort to understand different images and experiences of God presented by genuine devotees of different religious traditions has caused unresolved tensions. Of course these tensions can be avoided by not taking these people seriously, not seeking to know them further or not relating them to the one God, but this is an uncharitable approach.

Christians need to acknowledge the presence and work of God everywhere in the world, including in other religious and cultural traditions. We should value the genuine devotion, ethical values and liberative potentials found in people of other faiths. We may even call them the fruits of the Spirit, or signs of God's prompting. But how do we relate them to Jesus, whom the early Christians confessed as Lord, Christ and Saviour and who, in our view, provides a new orientation and centre for the whole of humanity? While some may feel that such questions are irrelevant today, the fact remains that believing in Jesus includes a distinctive image of God, a new orientation for humanity and a particular vision of the future. But this is not to say that we have possessed God, nor have we gained an exhaustive understanding of his nature and purpose for the history of humanity. Rather, we may feel with all humility that God has possessed us in some way through Jesus Christ. Precisely for this reason relating to people of other religions and understanding them as they are become indispensable for us.

Insights from scripture

What are the sources for guiding Christians to a right path of relating ourselves to people of other faiths? Do the scriptures help? Religious pluralism as it is today is a new phenomenon, and the writers of the Bible were not aware of it, though the Bible does provide some insights for dealing with it. Our Muslim friends, finding it difficult to give the status of scripture to the Bible, say that the holy Quran, as the last testament, supersedes it and gives a clearer answer for religious pluralism. According to it, although different nations have the freedom of having their own religions, the submission of the whole world to the will of Allah, as enshrined in the Shari'ah law, would be desirable. But Sikhs may claim that since their scripture *Adi Granth* is chronologically later than the Quran, it thus gives the final answer. The same may be the case with many other groups who consider the writings of their leaders as equal to scriptures.

The point is that this way of approaching the scriptures is not going to help in understanding religious pluralism. The place of scripture in religious life and in influencing attitudes towards people of other faiths differs from religious community to community. As Christians we consider the Bible to provide profound insights for a purposeful and meaningful life in a multi-faith context, focusing on Jesus as the centre, with the long Jewish prophetic tradition in which he stood and the new tradition that emerged after him. The insights of the Bible include appropriate attitudes to people of other faiths. Although it is not the purpose of this essay to deal with particular passages in the Bible, its overall perspective as a book of God's dialogue with human history through a chosen community will be reflected in the following discussion.

The scripture which the Christians call the Old Testament, if studied in its context, will reveal how the early Israelites appropriated complementary elements found in their neighbouring cultures, including the ideas of covenant, law, sacrifice, festivals, kingship, wisdom and the temple. The openness and creativity of these people are evident in how they gathered these elements around their own experience and commemoration of the exodus, which was central to their history and worship. At the same time, they were careful to reject certain gods and cults which promoted oppressive social, economic and political ideologies. Hence the tension between uniqueness and openness.

Jesus is the supreme example of commitment to God through a particular religious tradition and openness to people of other faiths. He moved among all kinds of people without any reservation and appreciated the extraordinary qualities of some of them, giving the name "faith" to their ability to transcend the existing norms and notions. But at the same time he was the greatest critic of religions. To a great extent his followers maintained this model, although those Christians who are exclusive and fundamentalist seem not to notice this. In fact by appreciating and appropriating the good values found among people regardless of their religious adherence, the church does no more or less than affirming one God, for "every generous act of giving, with every perfect gift, is from above, coming down from the Father of lights, with whom there is no variation or shadow due to change" (James 1:17). Further, new interpretative categories and points of contact may emerge from dialogue — whether in the first century when the writer of the fourth gospel used the term *logos* to explain the cosmic presence of the word which became flesh in Jesus, or in our own century when Christian theologians in India use Hindu categories to interpret Christian ideas.

Of course such a process of appropriating elements and establishing points of contact characterizes any religious tradition interested in relating its vision and ideals to other people. However, the conviction of Christians that Jesus Christ has become the centre is very important, as there are many centres proposed in the universe of faiths. This conviction may elicit an immediate negative reaction, because such convictions have tended to move towards totalitarian authoritarianism and absolute imperialism. Indeed, if Jesus is already viewed as a tribal god, ruthless conqueror and a king with arbitrary authority, such tendencies may be perpetuated. It is clear that this view is not absent from the Indian Christian scene, but it has also been consistently countered by thinkers who emphasize God's self-empty-ing and suffering as manifested in Jesus and his cross, and see the continued suffering of God symbolized in the crucified image of Christ as the antidote to self-centredness and imperialism. But they believe he alone can be an authentic centre for transforming the world; hence their voice for Christ-centred syncretism.

Plurality and contradiction

One of the greatest benefits of inter-religious dialogue is the clarifi-cation of our faith through listening to the questions of Hindus, Mus-lims and others. How then do we account for the irreconcilable differ-ence between the fundamental frameworks or core visions of different religions? To take the pluralist view, giving equal validity to all reli-gions, does not tackle this question adequately. In India religious plurality is often cited as an indirect justification of social and economic discrimination. Our appreciation of plurality must therefore be balanced by an acknowledgment of obvious contradictions.

The problem again lies in our view of the one God. God cannot contradict himself — unless one holds the view that consistency and contradiction in God's self-disclosure are beyond human intelligibil-ity, in which case we cannot evaluate any demand, including religious fanaticism and ethnic cleansing, that comes in the name of God or religion. Even those Indian monists (*advaitins*) who affirm that Reality is one, which may be realized at the final stage of the process of liberation by removing ignorance, will not subscribe to such a view, which undermines intelligibility and evaluation in the present world.

The common Hindu view that all religions are essentially the same seems, intellectually at least, to be the most convenient view for ordinary people. But when this issue is pushed further in dialogue there seems to be no consistent view of this common essence. Radhakrishnan claimed that all mystics speak the same language. But as far as we can read and understand, mystics of different religious traditions in fact speak different languages. Perhaps as a monist he is pointing to Reality beyond phenomenal and empirical appearances which are not ultimate, but this is obviously a distinctive position within the pan-mythic Hindu religious traditions. Some Hindus attribute the differences and apparent contradictions to the sport (*lila*) of God. But are sports arbitrary? It is interesting that Hindu thinkers are generally more concerned to counter the exclusive claims of the Semitic religions than to present their own distinctiveness.

Those who are familiar with the development of different religious traditions in India will easily recognize within them contrary perceptions and frameworks, including different understandings of God, world, human personality and goal. They seem not to be different ways to the same goal but different ways to different goals, as, for instance, the ritual, yogic and theistic traditions project them. Contemporary Hindu revivalists try to unify all Hindus in the name of cultural nationalism, but they pay no heed to contrary ontologies and cultic expressions. A deeper examination of their claims clearly discloses a strategy of reviving an ancient tradition with discriminatory social systems and ambiguous cultic practices which have been successively challenged by counter-movements. One element of this strategy is propagating the slogan that all religions are essentially the same, thereby upsetting those who appear to be distinctive and challenging.

Those committed to a particular vision of life find it difficult to understand the extraordinarily catholic outlook of average Hinduism, which for example allows theism, atheism, polytheism and monotheism as plausible positions. The Indian words for religion — *dharma* (comprehensive order) and *darsana* (vision) — are taken to stand for all-inclusive variety and contradictions. Of course, some Christians may be more inclusive than some committed Muslims, Sikhs, Jews and other Christians; yet if they are genuinely committed to the Christian vision and its requirements, their inclusivism is terribly limited by certain boundaries. But they cannot be easily criticized as narrow-minded, because there is authentic scope within their boundaries to love and respect other people with different visions and values.

Christian approaches to the people of other faiths cannot be confined to a Eurocentric viewpoint. Some of the slogans which have been presented as radically new from this point of view are not so for Indian Christians. The "Copernican revolution" in the theology of religions proposed by a few in the West, for example, is an old story for Indians. Certain Hindu thinkers repeatedly use the analogies of the sun and the hilltop and paths and sea and rivers to denote one God or Reality and many religions. The greatest struggle for Indian Christians is to convince their fellow-Indians that the gospel of Jesus Christ is something new and that it cannot be contained in old wineskins. And as a little flock of converts from the Hindu tradition, their position needs a more empathetic treatment by those Christians who reflect on religious pluralism elsewhere.

Commitment and openness

Out of this experience and reflection on it, some Indian Christians hold together commitment and openness with an unresolved tension. They do not wish to hide or trivialize their Christian commitment when they deal with religious pluralism. This does not mean that they are conservative or fundamentalist. In fact, after a long process of reflection about the New Testament and the tradition of the church, a few have gone so far as to bracket or even replace certain confessions and formulations of the Christian tradition by new versions more relevant to their context. But Jesus of Nazareth, a man who lived and died for others and who revealed to his followers the suffering love of God, continues to provide for them a field of force for living for others and living with hope. He and the traditions before and after him seem to have a distinctive vision for humanity and its fulfilment. He calls people to follow him expecting a response.

As those who have in some way responded to the call of Jesus even after the study of Indian religious traditions, these Indian Christians have never felt the need of giving it up. At the same time they are open to new visions and new calls should these be more profound and more meaningful. And even if they have no reason to go back to their original religion, they are open to liberative potentials in any religious tradition, and by mobilizing these they can work with others on proximate goals for a better life for people in India and elsewhere, leaving the question of ultimate goals for dialogue in due course. This is very important in a country so touched by continuing poverty and corruption. It stands to reason that we have to make the majority Hindu community in India see that they have a greater role to play in improving the living conditions of the people. It is not enough to boast of one's spiritual heritage without addressing social problems.

Between the extremes

Theologically, our approach to religious pluralism carries the unresolved tension between three sets of poles evident in the fundamentals of Christian faith.

1. *Grace and judgment.* Forgiveness and repentance are the bi-polar aspects of the gospel. According to the Bible, the primary nature of God is gracious. "The Lord is merciful and gracious, slow to anger and abounding in steadfast love" (Psalm 103:8). These words are repeated, in anger, by the prophet Jonah, who undergoes a conversion within a mission framework in relation to God's dealing with an "alien" people (Jonah 4:2). God's grace has reached out since creation to all humans through a myriad of channels, visible and invisible, in their cultures and religions. The grace and love revealed in Jesus openly attested to this. As God is gracious and forgiving, no Christian can restrict God from operating in his own way in all religions. As God has graciously tolerated religious pluralism, we as his children can only do the same. Even if we are sure that we are saved, we cannot boast, because it is by grace that we are saved (Ephesians 2:8).

On the other hand, along with Muslims, Christians affirm divine judgment, though on different scales. The judgment starts with the household of God, the church (1 Peter 4:17). As Christians themselves can deviate from the initiatives of God, so can every other religious person. God never overrules human freedom. Yet his call for repentance applies to all religions, whether or not one feels the need for it. As Jesus, one who preached repentance, did not deviate from God's will to the extent of dying the undeserved death of a criminal on the cross, God not only raised him from the dead and made him Lord but also will judge the whole world by him (Acts 17:31). Thus the Christian call for repentance addressed to all religious people is justified, but Christians are neither able to predict the response nor permitted to pass their own judgment.

2. *God as revealed and hidden.* Christians believe that God, who "spoke to our ancestors in many and various ways by the prophets", has spoken to us in these last days "by a Son, whom he appointed heir of all things, through whom he also created the worlds", and who is "the reflection of God's glory and the exact imprint of God's very being" (Hebrews 1:1-3). The New Testament interprets the significance of this revelation through various categories of religious thought, but the central perception of it is that God loves the world and because he loves he suffers. There are eloquent and elaborate descriptions of love in religious texts and cultural traditions, but its nature is most impressively defined on the cross, where God suffered through his son Jesus. Christians as children of God are expected to love their neighbours with nothing less than such suffering love.

At the same time there is the hiddenness of God. Why the God of suffering love allows different religious people to have a different feel and perception of him, we do not know. The promise of the Holy Spirit is to lead us into all truth. But this leading involves openness and struggle on our part just as it did for the prophets and Jesus. Now we know dimly, and in all humility we need to acknowledge the eschatological dimension of divine revelation. In the meantime our prayer and aspiration should be that, "rooted and grounded in love", we may "have the power to comprehend, with all the saints, what is the breadth and length and height and depth, and to know the love of Christ that surpasses knowledge", so that we may be "filled with all the fullness of God" (Ephesians 3:17-19). This is not the same as a pilgrimage of a mystery without any clue. The mystery has been revealed, and that is the ground for a continued comprehension of its fuller dimensions.

3. *Speaking and remaining silent.* For twenty centuries Christians have tried to understand theologically the plurality of religions. The various views set forth can be grouped under three headings: exclusive, inclusive and pluralist. Those who adopt the *exclusive* model — theologically or socially or both — view other religions as being at best human attempts to comprehend God, at worst demonic. It is not difficult to see that this view is uncharitable and unbiblical. Those who want to be *inclusive* see the theological worth of other religions, either as partial revelation or as having Christ, unknown or hidden, as

the real driving force of what is good and noble in each religion. Those who take a *pluralist* approach either relativize the place of each religion in the economy of divine reality or consider different religions as equally valid reflections of God's revelation through an amazing variety of ways or as moving together towards Reality.

It is not difficult to see these same models in the views of religious plurality held in other religions. In Hinduism, for example, the exclusive claims of Vedic religion have double strands. Socially and politically, the *brahmins* and *ksatriyas*, the ritualists and the rulers, have maintained mutual cooperation and superiority over the lower strata of society with religious justification. The worst sufferers have been the so-called outcastes, untouchables who are considered as impure. In terms of belief, the Vedic notion of ritual power, which is autonomously generated by performance according to strict procedures, is very distinctive. Moreover, there are two types of exclusivism. On the one hand, each orthodox school of Hindu philosophy establishes its own position and refutes the claims of others through arguments. On the other hand, the poet-saints of the devotional sects scarcely tolerate heterodox traditions like Buddhism and Jainism and even ridicule other devotional sects within the Hindu tradition. The polemic and persecution of other religious communities evident in the history of Hinduism have resulted from various combinations of these two strands.

Some of the sayings of Krishna in the *Bhagavad Gita* are among the best examples of Hindu inclusivism. Accordingly, in whatever way people approach God, he is accessible to them. He is the essence as well as the fulfillment of all their longings. In the modern period, the neo-Vedantins propose a ladder theory, according to which the experience of oneness with the supreme Reality is the topmost rung, while other religions and their experiences are placed on the lower rungs.

The pluralist view is often held on the basis of a single Vedic verse: "Truth is one and the wise call it by different names." A more commonsense version is that with which this essay began: that God is one and different religions worship him with different names and in different forms. It is not uncommon for Hindus to repeat the well-known Buddhist tale of six blind men who were told by the king to feel and describe an elephant. Each one felt only one part of the animal and described accordingly what an elephant is. Of course, those who use this analogy do not ask who the king is to see the elephant as whole. More interestingly, this tale is repeated to upset Christians and Muslims who come with absolute claims; otherwise, no committed Hindu would ever identify his or her religion with a blind man groping after partial truth. It is perhaps in order to escape the questions which can be raised about all three of the above positions that the theosophists declare that Truth is higher than all religions.

A pluralistic approach to pluralism

Aware of our identity as converts from another religion who for valid reasons cannot go back to it despite passionate calls to do so, we do not consider these three models as straitjackets. Things are much more complex. What is needed is a pluralistic approach to religious pluralism which is sometimes "exclusive", sometimes "inclusive" and sometimes "pluralist" in a certain sense — depending on the situation we are in and the kind of person we encounter. There are three basic reasons for taking this rather paradoxical position. In the first place, Judaism, Islam and Hinduism (to mention three examples) historically and conceptually relate to Christianity at different levels and to different degrees. Diverse sects within all these religions further multiply the levels and degrees. Second, Christians are admonished to discern the Spirit and discriminate between light and darkness. Although the "divine light" or "primordial seed" extends to every human, there are forces of darkness operating in religious traditions which may have different destructive manifestations. Third, we do not see all individuals, including Christians, as true representatives of the religions they profess. Our approach to and theology of religions thus depends on the particular contexts we are placed in and the particular individuals we encounter. This view may seem to be too individualistic, but the constant self-criticism provided by the Judaeo-Christian tradition can uphold it, and those who hold it need not be denied fellowship. On the other hand, when we see Jesus and his movement as unique and universally significant, we are in some way, at least indirectly, giving an inferior estimate to other great figures, their visions and their movements. Moreover, we find certain religious practices very ambiguous in terms of their worth and meaning. But if we talk about this openly, we may inflict deep wounds on the sensibilities of our partners in dialogue. As such, the best way of approaching religious pluralism is to be silent. Underneath this silence is a feeling of awesome wonder about the infinite wisdom of God's dealings throughout history and the whole of creation, as well as awareness and acknowledgment of our own finitude.

Finally, in a multi-faith context, we have the duty to understand others and the right to be understood ourselves. Bearing false witness against the other not only obstructs understanding but also goes against the truthfulness which is fundamental to a truly religious person. In India and elsewhere, untold transgressions have been and continue to be committed in this regard. Many begin their approach to other religions with foregone conclusions, without reaching out for introduction and discussion. In India interreligious ignorance has proved to be more horrible than any other ignorance.

We have to understand each other's religion, its origin, development and fundamentals, before we can take positions on religious pluralism. In the meantime we have to understand and accept others as they are. That may sometimes be difficult. For example, it is not easy to understand or accept one who subscribes to or legitimizes social oppression on the grounds of religion. On the other side, it may be terrifying for a Hindu or a Muslim to accept a committed Christian if he or she appears to be a missionary of a double (Judaeo-Christian) religious tradition. This need not be so if Christians repent of the terror they have created in multi-faith contexts and accept others as God's image even though they cannot approve of all that they say about God and the world. Their commitment and openness can find vivid expression only in the combination of a clear confession of faith and a sense of vulnerability.

Above all, people in a religiously pluralistic context need to learn that they can share their convictions authentically only in a dialogical mood created by friendship and cordiality. There is no need for any kind of locking horns.

One additional aspect in the process of dialogue is that the partners work for the continued transformation of their own religious traditions. As far as Christians are concerned, they need to recover the newness of the gospel and project it accordingly. This is indispensable for their self-understanding and communication. If we are really serious, we must work for a new reformation of the Indian church, radically questioning our structures and traditions.

Contributors

S. Wesley Ariarajah, a Methodist minister from Sri Lanka, is deputy general secretary of the World Council of Churches.

Rabbi **Elliot N. Dorff** is rector and professor of philosophy at the University of Judaism in Los Angeles, California.

Huang Po Ho, of the Presbyterian Church in Taiwan, is professor of systematic theology at Tainan Theological College and Seminary, Taiwan.

Rabbi **Maya Leibovic** is the spiritual leader of Congregation Mevasseret Zion, in the suburbs of Jerusalem. She was the first native-born Israeli woman to be ordained in Israel.

Chenfang Lo is professor of New Testament at Nanjing Union Theological College, and tutor of graduate students at the Centre for Religious Studies of Nanjing University, China.

Robert M. Seltzer is professor of Jewish history at Hunter College, New York, and the graduate school of the City University of New York, and director of the Hunter interdisciplinary programme in Jewish social studies.

Israel Selvanayagam, a minister of the Church of South India, teaches religions and is coordinator of the programme on interfaith dialogue at Tamilnadu Theological Seminary, Madurai, South India.

Rabbi Norman Solomon is fellow in modern Jewish thought at the Oxford Centre for Hebrew and Jewish Studies, and lecturer in the faculty of theology at the University of Oxford, England.

Hans Ucko, of the Church of Sweden, is an executive secretary in the World Council of Churches' Office on Interreligious Relations.

Wong Wai Ching Angela, an Anglican, is lecturer in the theology division of the Chinese University of Hong Kong.